# HEROES WITHIN

## A FRAMEWORK FOR EMPOWERING **STUDENTS** TO OWN THEIR LEARNING JOURNEYS

# AARON HANSEN

Solution Tree | Press

*a division of*
Solution Tree

555 North Morton Street
Bloomington, IN 47404
800.733.6786 (toll free) / 812.336.7700
FAX: 812.336.7790

email: info@SolutionTree.com
SolutionTree.com

Visit **go.SolutionTree.com/instruction** to download the free reproducibles in this book.

Printed in the United States of America

Library of Congress Cataloging-in-Publication Data

Names: Hansen, Aaron, author.
Title: Heroes within : a framework for empowering students to own their
   learning journeys / Aaron Hansen.
Description: Bloomington, IN : Solution Tree Press, [2024] | Includes
   bibliographical references and index.
Identifiers: LCCN 2023052902 (print) | LCCN 2023052903 (ebook) | ISBN
   9781945349546 (paperback) | ISBN 9781945349553 (ebook)
Subjects: LCSH: Student-centered learning. | Active learning. | Creative
   teaching. | Academic achievement.
Classification: LCC LB1027.23 .H365 2024  (print) | LCC LB1027.23  (ebook)
   | DDC 371.39/4--dc23/eng/20240208
LC record available at https://lccn.loc.gov/2023052902
LC ebook record available at https://lccn.loc.gov/2023052903

---

**Solution Tree**
Jeffrey C. Jones, CEO
Edmund M. Ackerman, President

**Solution Tree Press**
*President and Publisher:* Douglas M. Rife
*Associate Publishers:* Todd Brakke and Kendra Slayton
*Editorial Director:* Laurel Hecker
*Art Director:* Rian Anderson
*Copy Chief:* Jessi Finn
*Production Editor:* Madonna Evans
*Copy Editor:* Evie Madsen
*Cover Designer:* Rian Anderson
*Text Designer:* Fabiana Cochran
*Acquisitions Editors:* Carol Collins and Hilary Goff
*Assistant Acquisitions Editor:* Elijah Oates
*Content Development Specialist:* Amy Rubenstein
*Associate Editor:* Sarah Ludwig
*Editorial Assistant:* Anne Marie Watkins

# ACKNOWLEDGMENTS

I am deeply grateful for the many people who have been part of my journey of writing this book.

I am blessed to have more friends than I deserve, and their support and love through this process has been a beautiful and motivating gift. I must acknowledge two wizardly mentors and friends by name. For many years, Mike Mattos has consistently encouraged me to continue to step toward my potential in writing and speaking. Timothy D. Kanold is the other. Tim's generosity in sharing his knowledge and experiences about writing and life over deep dinner conversations is an irreplaceable treasure.

I am grateful for the entire Solution Tree Press team for helping to bring the ideas of the Hero-Maker Framework to a finished product and share it with the world. This team is by far the best in the business, and I am grateful for its support and commitment to me and my work. For me and so many others, Claudia Wheatley has been my advocate, cheerleader, and critic, all rolled into one. Her truthful yet kind feedback helped me find the path after getting momentarily lost in the weeds. This book wouldn't exist without the talented editor Amy Rubenstein. Her patience is remarkable as she reviewed, gave honest feedback, and helped me rethink the structure more times than I can remember. Madonna Evans is another editor who made this book what it is; she refined the rawness of my words while honoring my voice and message. I'm also grateful to Rian Anderson for creating a cover that communicates from beginning to end that this is a different kind of educational book.

To the students I've worked with in the past, the privilege you gave me of interacting with you and maybe being a small part of your journey still inspires me. To those students I don't know personally but see as I work with schools (many with eyes dulled with bored compliance or lack of hope), you are why I wrote this book. You inspire me to do better and speak boldly without fear. I am grateful to you for the message you send (without knowing it) to my heart and others' about your need for purpose. In you, I see so much beautiful potential. Without you, this book wouldn't exist. Thank you to the educators who are already wizardly in their purpose and efforts. So many of you have approached me—a stranger—willing to vulnerably share your stories and experiences, providing so much affirmation that I was on the right track.

Lastly, I am most profoundly grateful to my incredible family. You all have provided support, love, and encouragement in ways just as unique and beautiful as you each are. Thank you for choosing to be at our beautifully crowded table. I'm grateful to be part of your life's adventure. I love you.

Solution Tree Press would like to thank the following reviewers:

Lindsey Bingley
Literacy and Numeracy Lead
Foothills Academy Society
Calgary, Alberta, Canada

Davidson Blanchard
Curriculum Coordinator
Cambridge-Isanti Schools
Cambridge, Minnesota

Traci Logue
Assistant Principal
Lewisville Independent School District
Flower Mound, Texas

Christina Luce
K–8 Instructional Technology
Specialist
Liverpool Community School District
Liverpool, New York

Erica Martin
Literacy Coach
Kildeer Countryside School District 96
Buffalo Grove, Illinois

Jennifer Maulsby
School Improvement Specialist
Medford School District
Medford, Oregon

Carolyn Carter Miller
Educational Consultant
Fredericksburg, Virginia

Rebecca Nicolas
Assistant Principal
Fern Creek High School
Louisville, Kentucky

Janet Nuzzie
District Intervention Specialist, K–12
Mathematics
Pasadena Independent School District
Pasadena, Texas

Steve Pearce
Chief Human Resources Officer
Batavia Public schools
Batavia, Illinois

Christie Shealy
Director of Testing and Accountability
Anderson School District One
Williamston, South Carolina

Lauren Smith
Assistant Director of Elementary
Learning
Noblesville Schools
Noblesville, Indiana

Steven Weber
Assistant Superintendent
Fayetteville Public Schools
Fayetteville, Arkansas

# TABLE OF CONTENTS

# ABOUT THE AUTHOR

**Aaron Hansen** is a professional learning community (PLC) and response to intervention (RTI) expert and highly sought-after international speaker, strategic consultant, coach, and author. He has been featured on CNN, ABC, *FOX News*, and the BBC as an innovator and thought leader in U.S. education. As principal of a turnaround middle school, Aaron worked with staff and students to achieve to the highest, award-winning levels. He is the author of the book *How to Develop PLCs for Singletons and Small Schools*.

Aaron has knowledge and a track record of helping systems get results. He served on Solution Tree's PLC Advisory Board during PLC at Work© architect Richard DuFour's unfortunate battle with cancer. Aaron has a deep understanding for how to develop collaborative processes to help educators empower students through academic learning and has helped numerous educators dramatically transform their schools into high-performing systems.

To learn more about Aaron Hansen's work, follow @Aaronhansen77 on X, formerly known as Twitter.

To book Aaron Hansen for professional development, contact pd@SolutionTree.com.

# INTRODUCTION

## Stories, Journeys, Heroes, and Hope

**T**his book is about hope! It's about changing the trajectory of lives. It's about helping students each become the hero of their own story.

This book will help you empower learners to own their learning journey and their role in it, and in turn, direct their future. Too many students play the role of victim in their own story. Their experiences in school and elsewhere have them telling a story of feeling stuck. Students describe their existence in a system that's based on hoop-jumping compliance, with boring activities that don't apply to them or their world. So they bide their time, doing just enough to get by and keep their parents, teachers, or coaches off their backs—if they're lucky enough to have such adults in their lives. Many who don't, don't even try. Many students have a fixed mindset about their capabilities and who they are as learners. They think, "I'm no good at school. School isn't for me." This book is about changing *all* that.

This book introduces the six-step *Hero-Maker Framework*, which can help teachers build self-efficacy, engagement, and ownership of the learning journey in all students. The framework applies psychological and educational principles to help students reframe their thinking about their roles in school and life, and, even deeper than that, making them the *heroes* they are meant to be in their own stories. The framework will help you, the teacher, become a *hero maker*. The framework will help you create the right conditions to help your learners face real struggle and productively persevere. With your help, students will understand they are powerful enough to face—with quiet confidence—the inevitability of life challenges. They will know how to aim at something worthy of their effort, and how to work hard and pick themselves up and keep going when they get knocked down in the dirt. Essentially, that's all a *hero* is—someone who gets back up and keeps trying. By assuming the responsibility and role as their own capable hero, learners will be empowered with hope for a better future.

> *Essentially, that's all a hero is—someone who gets back up and keeps trying.*

The Hero-Maker Framework is about another kind of hope too. It's for educators who have felt the creep of burnout or frustration associated with feeling like they care more about student learning than the students or parents. It's for educators who have felt the sting of seeing their students' potential lying dormant and unrealized, and who so desperately want to help students realize that potential. This framework can help you have more influence on students while simultaneously managing to reduce the stress and overwhelm so prevalent among today's educators. This book will renew hope that you can and do make a profound difference in the lives of learners and the world.

This is a call to accept the responsibility of more definitively stepping into the two roles all educators play. The first role is as the *hero* of your own learning journey, both professionally and personally. The second role is that of a *wizard*, someone wise and powerful who helps others realize their own potential. Some tools in this book are for you as the learner, while others are for you (as a wizard) to use with your students.

Through the transformational experience of adopting the practices and principles of the Hero-Maker Framework, educators can revitalize their passion and hope for the profession, and experience the deep joy and fulfillment of knowing they are helping to change the trajectory of students' lives.

This book is intended for teachers, coaches, counselors, principals, school psychologists, social workers, and district-level leaders. Thoughtful parents could read and benefit from it too. Those who understand and use the steps in the framework can adapt the steps to empower students each to truly become the hero in their own learning journey!

# The Backstory

This book has many stories. People develop the deepest levels of understanding and more importantly, *meaning*, through stories. But it's not a book about *my* story. It's a research-based, practical guide for educators nested in stories. However, to really understand some of the important aims of this book and where the framework came from, I think it's helpful to know some of the backstory.

## My Call to Action

After a long board-member meeting at the White Pine School District boardroom in Nevada, I sat in the superintendent's office waiting for him to return. Moments before, he had turned on the light, ushered me in, and asked me to take a seat. I nervously fidgeted, racking my brain for what I might have done to be in trouble. I had been the assistant principal in our town's high school for a year. It was almost 10:00 p.m. The superintendent sat down heavily, seeming tired and impatient.

He stared into my twenty-eight-year-old eyes and said, "Aaron, I want you to be the principal of the middle school next year."

"Umm . . . OK," I stammered.

He went on, "The school's broken. You need to fix it." He paused to let that sink in and then said, "You have two years." That was the end of the meeting as I remember it. He may have said a few other things, but I don't recall them. All I heard was, "You need to fix it." The superintendent stood, shook my hand, told me, "We'll talk later," and turned off the light as we left the room. I was more than a little anxious as I drove home that night.

By virtually every metric, the middle school *was* broken: achievement was low, suspensions were high, and violence, bullying, high absenteeism, and high failure rates proliferated. Learning and the overall culture were in extremely poor condition.

That summer in 2006, as the newly appointed principal of White Pine Middle School, I scraped together the few school funds that we had, and six of my new teachers and I attended a Professional Learning Community (PLC) at Work© Institute. We were inspired! We had changes to make, and we knew it. Our students were suffering. Scared, but motivated, we went to work.

I could regale you with stories of our challenges (such as lack of funding, generational poverty, missteps and failures, and our own lack of knowledge or skills), but that's not what this book is about. The short version of this backstory is we did face some huge challenges, but we also began making serious and positive changes. We created a compelling shared vision and collectively committed to our agreed-on values. Other than our shared vision and values, we had little special skills or guidance. We messed up a lot, but we gave one another grace and continued to *fail forward*. Things got better.

Fast-forward three years to 2009, when the school was named one of approximately thirty model schools by the Center for Model Schools (formerly the International Center for Leadership in Education). Then, in 2011, the school was named national model middle school with the title *Middle School of Distinction*. We were also highlighted on AllThingPLC (www.allthingsplc.info) as a Model PLC school. Our school won many awards, and was featured in books, journal articles, news stories, a BBC documentary, on U.S. television, and more. Our school went from being one of the most "broken" schools in the United States to one of the most celebrated. The school was recognized for helping students grow academically, but more than that, the school staff were celebrated for building a positive, inclusive school culture serious about taking care of the whole student and celebrating growth.

The school was far from perfect, but it was exciting to see our efforts making a difference, and it was both humbling and flattering to receive so much attention. We were simply trying to do right by the students in our classrooms. But what people don't know is that as we got better and better results and the recognitions continued to come, we were also experiencing more and more frustration. Yes, we had made significant gains, but we felt like we were pulling teeth to get students to learn, particularly with our many students who struggled. Although they needed our help the most, they also resisted it the most. Many of these students simply weren't interested in complying with our efforts.

We knew we were not going to reach our vision of every student truly learning at high levels if we continued doing what we were doing. Also, we knew we couldn't sustain our current level of effort. We were on the path to burnout! We knew that, even as one of the most celebrated schools in the United States at the time, something was fundamentally wrong. Our students felt it too and resisted being "forced" to learn, feeling as if school were being *done to them*. I also knew we were not alone. I encounter these sentiments from educators almost everywhere I go, and increasingly so since the

COVID-19 pandemic. One particular experience with a student made the pain point crystal clear for me.

## A Story About Cody

Fast-forward to October 2012. Cody, an eighth-grader, sat in my office after the teacher kicked him out of class. Cody and I had many talks over the previous two years. His parents had been in and out of jail, and protective services had been involved. He was late to school every day. Cody was smart, but struggled academically and with his behavior. I tried to understand the complexity of Cody's situation, and I had worked hard to build a positive relationship with him. So, per one of the programs in the school at the time, I had "adopted" Cody as one of *my* kids. We had a real relationship, not just a "you're in trouble" relationship.

On this day, he was in trouble. I invited Cody to sit down across from my desk and asked, "Cody, why are you here?"

Slouching low in his chair, with arms crossed, and a scowl on his face, he responded, "I dunno. Teacher doesn't like me."

I sighed and said it again, "Come on, Cody, why are you here?"

"I dunno!"

I sighed again, stood up, and walked the short distance down the hall to his mathematics intervention class.

As I stepped in, I felt the tension in the room hit me in the face like a gust of wind. I walked over to the teacher (a good teacher), and asked gingerly, "Hey . . . so Cody's in the office? What's going on?"

She put her hands on her hips and spoke without a filter. "I'm trying to help these kids, but I feel like nothing's working. I'm giving my all, and they simply don't care! See all these boys?" She swept a finger in the direction of a group of what most teachers would consider *challenging students* without looking. "Well, Cody is the ringleader of this circus, and his currency is all about making them laugh!" She pointed her finger right at my face and said through clenched teeth, "I just needed a break, Aaron!" I raised my hands in surrender. I felt my neck get hot as my frustration rose. I told her I would talk with Cody. She agreed I could send him back to class when he was ready, and that class was where he needed to be, but—again with the finger pointing—"He better be ready!"

By the time I made it back into my office, I was more agitated. I asked my question again, "Cody, why are you here? Why aren't you taking this seriously?" He sighed and rolled his eyes, just as tired of this dance as I was. I lectured him about things like being accountable for behavior and taking responsibility for his learning. I could see he was getting frustrated too. I asked my question again, "Cody, why are you here?" By now, he was scowling with anger, and he sat up. I thought, *Good! At least I'm going to get some kind of reaction out of you.*

He looked me square in the eyes and hissed through clenched teeth, "What does it matter?"

Hoping we might now be able to have a real conversation, I asked softly, "What do you mean, Cody?"

Through gritted teeth, he said words that hit me so hard, they would forever change my life. He simply said, "What does it matter? 'Cause I'm never . . . getting . . . outta . . . here!" With each word, his finger jabbed the air toward my chest. I felt it like a punch.

I sat there silently. What could I say? The moment wasn't lost on me. I knew what he meant. He didn't mean he was never getting out of mathematics intervention, a class he'd been in for more than two years. What he meant was, "I'm never getting out of my crappy life." Time froze; I felt it—his hopelessness, despair, and belief he was destined to repeat familial patterns. He silently fell back into his chair, looking down to hide the tears welling. At thirteen years old, he had already given up hope for his life and his future. What do you say in that moment? There are no sufficient words.

I sat quietly in my awkwardness and then filled the silence. I wanted him to see what I saw in him: that funny and illusive but real thing called *potential*. I gave my best attempt at a pep talk, one he'd probably heard a million times. I spoke kindly and lovingly. I felt as helpless as he did, like an impostor, inadequate in the moment. He sat compliantly, but not really hearing or believing my vision of his potential. Why would he? He had at least two years of evidence showing he was not a strong learner, and that was just in mathematics. Finally, not knowing what else to do, I pleaded, leaning on our relationship, "Cody, for me, please, will you go back to class? Will you *please* try to learn this? No more problems with your teacher, OK? Please!" He nodded and went back to class and didn't have any more problems—for a while. I wanted to scream. That moment hurt.

What had become so abundantly clear to me was I could see potential in Cody he couldn't see in himself. He didn't believe in himself. And as much as he trusted me, my belief wasn't enough to counter his self-limiting one, formed over years of experience, that he "was never getting outta here!" It didn't matter what I said; Cody only believed the story in his head.

Have you ever experienced a similarly frustrating situation? Have you ever seen so much more potential in your students than they see in themselves? My guess is you have. That's why this book is for you. I felt completely helpless against a challenge I had no idea how to face, and it wasn't just Cody. Staff at my school witnessed this disengagement, disenfranchisement, forced compliance, frustration, and apathy in so many students—and not just in those learners struggling with grades or achievement. It seemed the harder we tried, the harder students resisted. It was overwhelming and part of me wanted to quit, to find something easier to do with my life where the stakes were not as high.

Cody had what psychologist and professor Carol S. Dweck (2006) famously and simply describes as a *fixed mindset*. People with a fixed mindset believe their abilities and talents are fixed or unchangeable. People with a fixed mindset usually avoid challenges and give up easily, which limits their growth and opportunities (Dweck, 2006). It's a simple term, but it's not a simple thing to change. I knew it wasn't just Cody and the other students in intervention, but Cody gave me a place to start. I began trying to figure out where these fixed mindsets were coming from. I came to understand that educators and school systems are a big part of the problem. Educators and school systems can unintentionally condition students like Cody to believe their ability as learners is unchangeable. Their repeated failures become evidence for the story they tell themselves.

## Fixed Mindsets and Other Negative Beliefs

Imagine you're a learner repeatedly pulled into small groups—or worse, out of class—starting as early as first grade. There's nothing wrong with small groups if they actually help. But too often, students who get pulled out of class don't really get better, or their improvement is so slow students can't see it themselves (Hattie, 2009). Because they don't get better, their situation doesn't change. If you're that student, you'll subconsciously start to say to yourself, "There are the learners, over there, and then there's me, over here." In other words, "I'm not a learner." If educators poorly diagnose a learning deficit or poorly design or execute the intervention, it won't work.

Ability grouping has long-term negative effects on students' academic trajectory and attitudes toward learning in general (Hattie, 2023). Students in the lower tracks often experience lower self-perceptions and diminished confidence compared with their peers in higher tracks (Hattie, 2023). The continued pattern of being pulled out becomes hard evidence for a story, which is simply the mind's attempt to make meaning out of an experience. The *experience* is being pulled repeatedly. The *meaning* attached to the experience is "I'm not a learner." It's not a true story, but if told enough times, the person telling it will believe the story. Once students believe the story, they act out, producing further evidence for the story; it's a reinforcing loop. Eventually an identity forms, rooted in a self-limiting fixed mindset. They are no longer learners who are struggling, they become struggling learners. It's *who* they are. This is why educators, as professionals, must be precise in their language. They must describe students' current position, not them. Otherwise, educators inadvertently label students and give them further evidence for a self-limiting story and identity.

Experiences educators provide in their school systems condition many learners to believe they are non-learners. These students come to this conclusion by what is in their mind: vast amounts of evidence of failure. They often begin to feel like victims of a system intended to help them. That's when educators start to see these subconscious feelings manifest outwardly as disengagement, avoidance, anger, frustration, off-task behaviors, discouragement, or—most insidiously—apathy.

The same behaviors show up for students with a fixed mindset who don't struggle, but cannot see *relevance* in the learning. More subtle is a whole host of other students who are simply enduring school, compliantly doing just enough to get by, but not truly engaged or owning their learning. These students use language to describe their experience similar to the language of minimum-security prison inmates, who compliantly say they are "doing time." They have the occasional privilege to look forward to, but their sights are set on the future, when they "get out" into the "real world." I realized these attitudes were not held just among a small minority of our middle school students, but instead resonated with most students. And it's getting worse. I'll explain why in chapter 2 (page 35). Students shouldn't feel this way.

Thus began my quest to help. I felt called to understand why students felt this way, and what we (as educators) needed to do to change the circumstances leading to the negative mindsets so many of our students had about school or themselves. I wanted to make our school a place where all students held the belief that they are truly capable, and what they were doing mattered and empowered them. It would be more complicated than simply praising effort versus achievement, as much of the popular literature suggested at the time (Gross-Loh, 2016). It wasn't about a new program or software or behavior initiative. We'd already done those things, at award-winning levels! This was deeper.

With teachers I trusted, we started experimenting. We read about intervention and mindset. We paid attention and noticed what worked and what didn't. We failed, reflected, and learned. We started sharing what we were doing with other educators. Slowly, we started to shift the onus of control and empowerment more to students. We became intentional, not just in the development of student academic skills but also the attributes of self-efficacy.

We started by targeting students in intervention, but later worked with students at the higher end of the achievement spectrum. Then we expanded our focus to everyone in between. We had success. Our interventions and even regular classes began to shift. Students were more engaged and empowered, and achievement scores reflected the shift. The ancillary benefit we didn't anticipate was that the stress, fatigue, and feelings of burnout in our teachers started to melt away. But by far more impactful to me than the improved scores was that we were starting to become intentional in helping our students believe in themselves and take ownership of their role in their learning journey.

## The Hero's Journey

My quest to understand how to empower students continued even after the seven years I served as principal of White Pine Middle School. By then, I had begun presenting what my staff and I had learned about principles of empowerment and changing mindsets at institutes, conferences, and on district and school professional development days. I shared tools and success stories with thousands of educators. People were moved and deeply inspired, and often approached me after the sessions to share their own stories, with tears or hugs. They would tell me how their own lives had been changed by that *one teacher who empowered them* or how they got to be that *one teacher* for one of their learners.

That my message resonated so deeply and profoundly with fellow educators was exciting, but a frustration began to brew in me. Over time, it became abundantly clear to me that even though I had inspired educators and they wanted to take action to empower their learners, they really didn't know what to do when they got back to their classrooms. I didn't have a reliable way to help teachers replicate their own successes. I knew these concepts worked, but I didn't know *how* to help others understand the underlying psychological principles at a level deep enough so they could take the tools and adapt them to their own situations and to individual students in a doable way. I needed a more concrete framework to empower teachers with a clear set of steps to follow with their students.

I decided maybe I needed a deeper understanding of the principles first. I left behind the contemporary literature and started reading the works of some classic educational and psychological thinkers, including Albert Bandura (1977, 1997), Carl G. Jung (1954, 1980), Abraham H. Maslow (1943), Jean Piaget (1932), Carl R. Rogers (1951, 1961), Lev S. Vygotsky (1986), and others. I spent years reading books and listening to podcasts on topics such as human motivation, drive, and psychological development and change, all seemingly unrelated to education.

Then, in what I can only describe as divine inspiration, I stumbled across the work of writer and literature professor Joseph Campbell (1949) and his description of the narrative framework he calls *the hero's journey*. This was it!

*The hero's journey* is Campbell's (1949) description of the archetypal patterns that show up in so many of the world's myths and stories at the foundation of societies. Leaning heavily toward Jungian archetypes, Campbell (1949) explains the pattern: a would-be hero feels an inner call to adventure, then usually an unseen force gives the hero a glimpse of their true potential. The hero meets a mentor or guide who offers wisdom when it's most needed. The hero faces tests and difficult challenges, and ultimately their own fears. They eventually overcome what at first seemed to be unsurmountable difficulties, and return transformed—more capable, wiser, and better able to benefit their community or the world at large (Campbell, 1949).

I began to understand how many of the classic stories built our collective culture and follow the patterns. These themes are buried so deep in our consciousness, we don't even notice them. Swiss psychiatrist and psychoanalyst Carl G. Jung (1954) calls these assumptions the *collective unconscious*. How often the hero's journey was part of our contemporary world also fascinated me. It seemed like nearly every popular book or movie had elements of Campbell's (1949) hero patterns (like *Star Wars*, the Harry Potter series, *King Arthur*, *The Lion King*, *Lord of the Rings*, *The Avengers*, and more). Once I saw the patterns, I couldn't unsee them; they are everywhere!

Take the classic film I grew up watching, *Star Wars*. Director George Lucas attributed the deep resonance with audiences to the film's close adherence to the work of Campbell (1949) and the hero's journey (as cited in BillMoyers.com Staff, 1999). The plot illustrates the hero's journey. Character Luke Skywalker believes he is destined for a dusty, dull existence. Through trying circumstances, he's awakened to the idea that maybe he's meant for more. He answers what Campbell (1949) terms the *call to adventure*; Luke feels that call from an unseen *force*. Luke makes many mistakes in his development as he trains and learns, mostly because he struggles to believe in himself.

As part of his development, Luke meets wise mentors along his path. One of them is Yoda, who sees potential in Luke that Luke can't see in himself. Fully capable himself, Yoda doesn't solve Luke's problems or steal his journey. Instead, Yoda motivates Luke by having his pupil complete a series of challenges that help Luke develop his skills and start to recognize and believe in his own potential. A turning point in Luke's development is when he must face his fears—something everyone must do in life to realize their potential. At the direction of his mentor, Luke goes into a dark cave or, in Campbell's (1949) terms, "the belly of the whale." There Luke faces his deepest fears, which are his own temptations, weaknesses, and frailty—universal fears all people share. This transformative moment allows Luke to emerge with a little more courage and self-awareness, and he can humbly step into his new role with a quiet confidence. He is ready to face the challenges ahead as he walks toward his purpose as a hero. With no guarantee of success, Luke assumes responsibility for himself, the welfare of his remaining family members and friends, and ultimately the future existence of the entire galaxy.

Our lives are not so fantastical, but in essence, what Campbell (1949) figured out is we are all on the hero's journey, called to the adventure of a life meaningfully lived. We are all given the opportunity to face fears, learn, stumble, and grow while we work to transform into who life needs us to be to make things better for ourselves, our families, and our communities. All people are heroes in their own story, and that's why stories matter so much. Whether we know it or not, stories are about us.

> *We are all on the hero's journey, called to the adventure of a life meaningfully lived.*

## The Power of Stories

Through this exploration, I began to even more deeply understand the importance of stories—particularly stories about journeys—to organizations, cultures, and most importantly, individuals. This includes metaphorical journeys of transformation that love stories often depict. All the best stories are about struggle, challenge, and personal transformation. *Star Wars* may not be your jam, but at some point a story resonated with you or moved you on a deep level. It did so because whether you knew it or not, you saw something in the hero's journey that reminded you of *you*. You are the hero in your own story.

I had already recognized that stories matter to organizations. For years, I had cited renowned educator and best-selling author Roland S. Barth's work. As a school culture expert, Barth (2001) said, "cultures are defined by the stories we tell ourselves" (p. 5). Barth is right, and Campbell showed me why. Countries, communities, tribes, and even families define what they value, their culture, and ultimately who they are through the stories they tell (Geertz, 1973). Stories are foundational to people's perceptual understanding of existence and their place in life. Stories breathe life into beliefs and declarations of values. Stories are powerful!

I started to apply these broad ideas to students and why some of them see themselves as victims instead of the heroes they are meant to be. Coauthors Byron Katie and Stephen Mitchell (2008) gave me insight into *why* unexamined thoughts often lead a person to create narrative interpretations about events, people, or current, past, and future situations: "The whole world is simply my story, projected back to me on the screen of my own perception. All of it" (p. 36). Each story is a reflection of a thought the person believes. Unchecked, people also define conceptions of self through the stories they tell themselves *about themselves*. These thoughts, especially repetitive ones, create your perception of your identity—who you believe yourself to be in the world. This simply means you tend to believe the repeated thoughts you have about yourself, and if unquestioned or unchecked, you will subconsciously act out those beliefs, just like a character in a story.

Tell yourself "I'm no good at math" long enough and you'll believe it. Once you believe it, you'll act it out, proving your story right. Act out the story long enough and it becomes your *default programming* that runs every time a similar situation arises.

Eventually, you'll even attach your identity to it, believing this is *who* you are. Telling yourself "I'm no good at math," unchallenged, can eventually equate to "I'm no good at math, and I'm simply not capable. It's not in my DNA to be able to learn it." Voilà! Now you're a victim of bad genes, life, or circumstances. Regardless, you've given away your power, all because you believed your self-limiting thoughts and a story over which you had no influence.

But, if stories can create negative self-beliefs, stories can also create positive ones! Change the story, change the mindset. Change the mindset, change the outcome. This was it! Could educators help students tell new stories where learners' failures and mistakes were simply stepping stones toward success, just like in the hero stories? Could educators challenge the feelings of victimhood students create after years of conditioning in a compliance-based system? Could students intentionally develop the quiet, humble confidence of heroes through specific and repeatable practices? Could educators harness the power of the hero's journey patterns so deeply embedded in the psyche of every individual in society? Could educators help students tell better stories about themselves? The answer to all of it is, without question, *yes!*

From there, the Hero-Maker Framework became crystal clear and fell into place. Educators can change the way they approach learning. They can help students change their stories, empowering them with the ownership of learning essential academic skills. Using the power of the hero's journey, I created a step-by-step framework grounded in educational best practices, along with guiding psychological principles. This framework helps teachers reliably and repeatably empower students to trade in a fixed mindset (or a compliance-based mindset) for a mindset where students each see themselves as the hero of their learning journey. Providing this doable framework will also help teachers on their own transformational journey, and allow them to step into their rightful role as people who inspire. They would be the Merlins to King Arthur, the Dumbledores to Harry Potter, and the Yodas to Luke Skywalker, the powerful and wise wizards who help their learners see their true potential. No more victims, only heroes taking ownership of their journey, fulfilling their limitless potential. Could teachers move from being deliverers of content to something much grander? They could become nothing less than providers of hope. This is big and could change countless lives of young learners and careers of adults.

# The Hero-Maker Framework

This is when the telling of my story about my journey ends for now and yours begins. In this book, I lay out the six-step Hero-Maker Framework that teachers, coaches, parents, schools, and district leaders can follow to help learners become the hero of their own learning journey. Few of the educational principles I describe in this book are new; in fact, most are old. Many foundational thinkers in education got it right the first time. What is new is the framework of concrete steps anchored in deep psychological principles and today's cultural conditions.

I designed these practical educational steps to facilitate a shift from the compliance-based experience so many students endure, to a new story about perseverance, accomplishment, reflection, self-efficacy, and ultimately, becoming the hero of their own learning journey. As the phrase goes, *change your story, change your life*. But make no mistake, this book isn't about positive self-talk. It's about providing students with new experiences as a basis for intentionally creating a new accompanying story about who they really are.

The Hero-Maker Framework can help educators shift their currency from content and standardized test scores to becoming brokers in hope, personal power, and the fruition of dreams. Using this framework leads to deeper levels of academic learning too. The framework will help teachers show their students a glimpse of their true potential and empower students to become the heroes in their own journey, where they take ownership of learning essential academic skills and also new personal dispositions that will serve them throughout their lives. Using this framework can change the trajectory of students' lives and the lives of their future families. It has the potential to completely redefine the purpose of education. And your work and your story in that transformation matter! You are the key. The steps of the framework can be seen in figure I.1 and are detailed in the chapter descriptions in the next section.

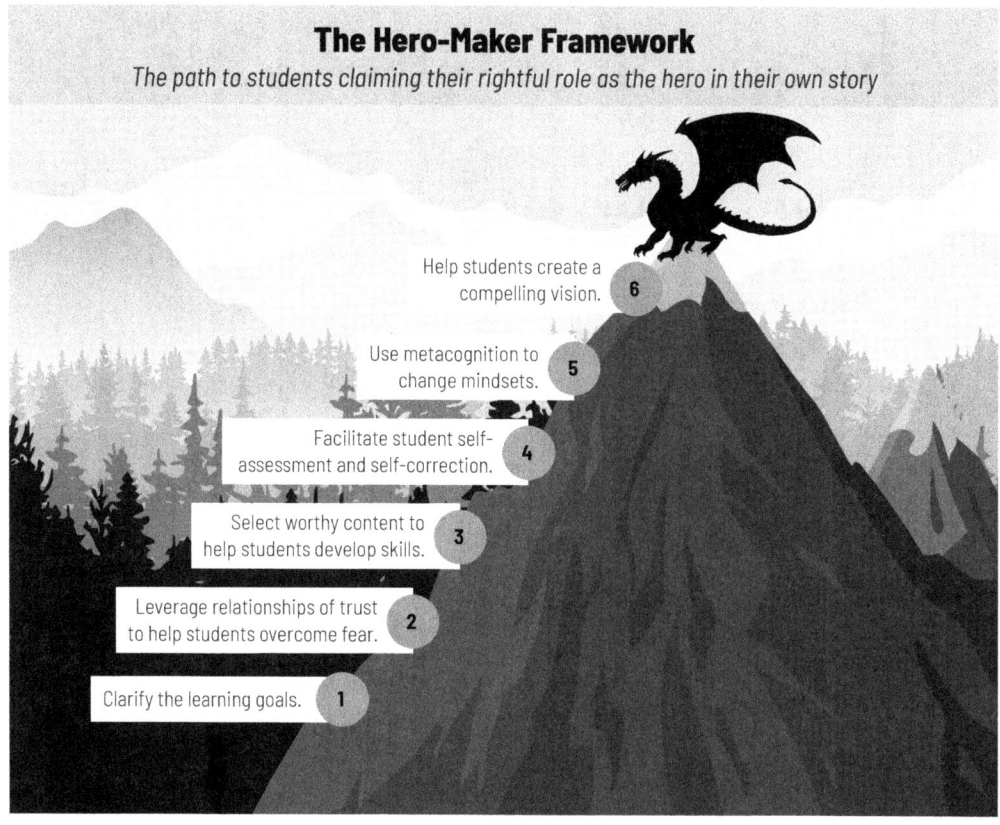

**FIGURE I.1:** The six-step Hero-Maker Framework.

## About This Book

This book is for any adult (or team of adults) who desires to impact learners in the most meaningful and life-changing way possible. It's for those who trust that self-belief plus effort and time impact destiny. This book provides a systematic, repeatable, and doable framework for encouraging self-belief in each student those believers serve.

I will explain the six steps of the framework in depth in each of the first six chapters.

» Chapter 1 explains the need for would-be heroes (learners) to see and understand the learning goal. For learners to take ownership of their learning journey, they must clearly see what the destination looks like.

» Chapter 2 explains the psychological reasons people shy away from challenges at times, and the fears behind their reluctance. This chapter goes into depth about how educators (as wizards) can develop credibility and garner trust so potential heroes believe their encouragement.

» Chapter 3 explains why it's necessary to provide relevant, real-world learning worthy of a hero's efforts. I also explore why choice is paramount for this generation to engage.

» Chapter 4 explains the difference between *directive feedback* and *facilitated feedback*. It shows examples with dialogue and offers scripts for helping students self-assess, track their progress, and self-select course corrections on their learning journey.

» Chapter 5 explains how to help learners metacognitively reflect on their tracked progress for developing self-efficacy and changing their story about themselves.

» Chapter 6 illustrates why students need a vision for their future. This chapter also explains the role educators play in helping students create, believe in, and take their vision seriously.

» Chapter 7 helps teachers and teams get started. It provides guidance in the development of tools teachers need to implement the Hero-Maker Framework.

There are steps within the steps, and I provide ample examples and tools. That said, the concepts are not simple. They interweave so much at times it's impossible to separate them. There is also some repetition of concepts from one chapter to the next to purposely help the reader more deeply learn the framework. While the reader must understand the principles embedded in the practices to adapt to each individual learner, the framework gives a pattern educators can follow with every learner. I intentionally use stories to illustrate the principles because stories are important for people to understand things deeply. Please note, I have changed some names in the stories for privacy.

No less significant are journeys. A journey is perhaps the most prolific metaphor people use, especially when trying to explain important changes or learning in life. Try to explain your life, especially changes you've made, without using words or phrases like *journey* or *my path*. The reason is because on a journey, you start one place and end up somewhere different, hopefully somewhere ultimately better. That's the hope of under-taking a journey, that things will be better on the other side of it. Journeys are about *hope*. There's an element of hope in every journeyer. Some learners desperately need a hopeful journey; it represents hope for something better. Some of you do too. Where possible, I encourage teachers to take this journey of learning these concepts with their book clubs and collaborative teams. Journeys are better together. They are usually easier and faster together too. But if you don't have a team, don't let that stop you!

The Hero-Maker Framework teaches you how to help your learners have enough courage to step on the path and begin the journey to realize their potential. It helps learners assume their rightful role as the hero in their own learning journey. However, learning the framework and using it empowers you too! For many adults, the framework represents those supporting the development of a new opportunity to go on their own learning journey—a journey where they can aim at a loftier vision than before, more in line with why they became teachers in the first place.

So with love I encourage you to step toward the unknown of *your* potential. Transcend the role (an old story tells you) of yourself just being a deliverer of content, dealing in the currency of standardized test scores, and instead write a new story where you become something more: a bringer of hope, a hero maker. It's your calling; it's what you were made to do. Otherwise, you wouldn't be reading this book. Your work matters, and you are more powerful than you realize!

Journeys are never without serious challenges—even real risk. I honor the battles you will face as you lead the way, challenging traditional mindsets and institutional structures, and the hurt of inevitable failure that comes with all journeyers before the moments of triumph. I deeply respect the vulnerability it takes to step into the unknown of your own potential as you try to change things significantly for the better. My heart swells with gratitude as you attempt to bring hope to the hopeless and build a new generation of journeyers and heroes, powerful beyond comprehension. Take care of your fellow travelers, and good luck on your journey!

# CHAPTER 1

# Clarify the Learning Goals

**The Hero-Maker Framework**

*The path to students claiming their rightful role as the hero in their own story*

Clarify the learning goals. ①

**P**eople have five senses: sight, hearing, touch, taste, and smell. Through those senses, people experience the world and have a need to make meaning about many experiences. As I discuss in the introduction (page 1), one way to make meaning is through telling stories about those experiences. The story you tell yourself *about* yourself ends up becoming something you believe. When you believe it, you subconsciously act it out, proving you are right. When you act it out, it becomes habituated as default programming for future experiences (Katie, 2007).

So if educators are going to truly help empower students to permanently own their learning journey, part of their role must be helping some students change the story they tell themselves about their role in school and learning. If you want to help students change their stories, how do you do that in a practical, real-world, boots-on-the-ground way? The short answer is to start by crafting experiences that will give students new evidence for a new story.

The first step to empowering students to be the hero of their own learning journey is simple. They must actually know *what it is they're supposed to learn*. If you're going to be in charge of your journey, you have to know where you're going! If not, you're simply a tourist at the mercy of a guide. In educational terms, teachers must ensure students understand what the essential outcome or learning goal should look like when they reach proficiency. Teachers need to become better—in fact, exceptional—at communicating the intended learning goals to students. This requires intentionality, and goes way beyond simply posting objectives or standards on the board. This step is especially important for students who struggle with fixed mindsets or motivation, but it is applicable for every student.

Educators know the power of communicating the intended learning goals to students; research supporting this goes all the way back to the 1950s (Bloom, Englehart, Furst, Hill, & Krathwohl, 1956). Researcher and author Robert J. Marzano (2009) explains that student achievement gains are roughly 1.2 standard deviations greater when teachers communicate the learning goals than when they don't communicate them. Professor and academic researcher John Hattie (2009) weighs in, "The most powerful way to increase students' achievement is to have them deeply involved in their own learning" (p. 29). You must know the goal to be deeply involved, right?

Because of the preponderance of evidence of the benefits of clear learning goals, every worthy observation tool, clinical supervision tool, or formal teacher evaluation process should include whether the teacher is communicating the intended learning goals. Often, efforts to address this highly overlooked principle of empowerment end up getting a half-hearted nod from a supervisor when the teacher posts an objective on the board. Teachers often only do this as an act of compliance with administrative evaluation expectations. But this won't cut it! If your goal is to empower students to take ownership of their learning, they must know—in clear terms—what you expect them to learn. And, for them to know what it is they're supposed to learn, teachers must be clear about the goals first! That's not easy. It's a process that takes a lot of work for teachers to really be clear about the intended learning goals in any given grade level or class.

# Students Must Understand the Learning Goal

It's good that teachers work to get clear on learning goals, but there is almost always a significant stakeholder group left out of this process. These stakeholders are often underestimated and given truly little responsibility for ensuring learning. See if the following scenario is familiar.

I step into a classroom, wait for an opportune time to talk to a student, and ask, "What are you supposed to learn today?" Although the learners' responses vary a bit (based on age, for example), most often in a typical classroom, the student responds without real words, but with a series of guttural grunts, shoulder shrugs, and the occasional, "Uh . . . I dunno."

Sometimes the response to my question is much more promising. After asking my question, the student looks at my face and, with a head rotating like it's on a swivel, the learner reads the objective the teacher has written on the board. When this happens, I'm excited! It's obvious the teacher has made efforts to help communicate the learning goal to the students! I show my genuine excitement and then ask my follow-up question: "That's awesome! Can you tell me what that means?" Guess what happens most often? Yep, you guessed it! They don't know. Sometimes students, when asked what they are supposed to learn for the day, will just start to explain the activity, "You're supposed to take these names over here and you match them with this stuff over here." I'm always supportive, "Wow! That sounds amazing! So can you tell me what you're supposed to *learn* by doing that activity?" I can hear crickets in the silence as the student tries to figure it out.

The point is students are often just "doing school." They are dutifully putting in their time, doing the work, and complying with what the teacher says. But they do not intentionally focus on using the experiences their well-meaning teachers provide to learn in an intentional and purpose-driven way. Students may be able to parrot the objective on the board, but often, they don't really understand the intended learning goal. Without knowing the learning goal, how can they own it?

When speaking with large groups of educators about student ownership, I often ask a provocative question to start the conversation: "How can you expect students to truly take ownership of their learning if they don't know what they are supposed to learn?" But I also ask them to really consider my question and any potential implications the answer might have for their practice. Most educators nod thoughtfully and discuss with a peer. Some get a little defensive. I follow up, "Do your students know what they are supposed to learn? Can students point at something and say, 'That's where I'm going on this learning journey. That's what my work will look like when I know how to do this skill'"?

> *To take ownership of accomplishing a goal, you have to first know what the goal is.*

I explain, "It's kind of like having a destination on a map. Do you remember those old-school paper things before GPS that always ended up stuffed in the glove compartment or lying on the floorboards of cars?" Digital or paper, a map is a useful tool. However, a map is absolutely useless if you don't know where you're trying to go. To take ownership of accomplishing a goal, you have to first know what the goal *is*. You must be able to *see* it.

## Why Communicating the Learning Goal Is So Important

Imagine *archery* is an essential skill and you want to learn how to do it. In collective history, archery may well have been an essential skill for you and your family as a means for getting food. If you weren't proficient with a bow, you didn't eat. Not so today, but let's pretend archery is an essential skill, and as someone who doesn't have this essential skill, you want to learn. Let's consider two different scenarios for learning archery.

### Scenario One

Whether you've done archery before or not, imagine you're new to it. You're serious about learning it, so you get a teacher. Your teacher takes you into a dark room, turns the lights completely out, blindfolds you, hands you a bow and an arrow, and says, "There's a target in that general direction over there." You can't see the target, but your teacher assures you one is over there and says, "Take a shot at the target." Most people were raised to be compliant, so you do what you're told, hope no one is over there, and let an arrow fly. Of course, you miss the target. Archery is difficult, especially when you can't even see what you're aiming at!

Your teacher says, "Oh, that was too high. This time aim a little lower." Still blindfolded, you shoot again. Your teacher tells you it was too low, and to aim a little higher. "That was too much to the left." Compliantly, you do what you're told. You take the feedback you receive and keep trying. There's no fulfillment of progress toward the goal. Why? Because you can't see the target, nor can you see your performance in relation to the target. This process would be beyond boring, perhaps frustrating too.

Let's say that after a while you do actually get lucky and hit the target. Your instructor praises you to the moon: "You hit it! Great job! Way to go! Here's a prize!" You enjoy the praise (because praise feels good), but whose accomplishment is it really? Yours or the teacher's? Who performed the cognition of adjusting to *hit* the target? You were just a machine, performing the act, compliantly doing what you were told. Because it wasn't really your accomplishment, there's no sense of true ownership, gratification, or fulfillment.

## Scenario Two

Now imagine that you're in that same dark room and you're holding the bow and arrow. Then, your teacher takes off your blindfold, turns on all the lights, and asks, "Do you see that target over there?" You see it, nod, and say, "Yes." Your teacher isn't satisfied with that answer and says, "No, do you see it over there, that round thing?" "Yes," you reply again. Your teacher annoyingly points it out again, "Do you see? It's that round thing with the rings and red dot in the center." Feeling frustrated with this redundancy, you say, "Yeah, I got it! I really see it!" Satisfied, your teacher says, "OK, see if you can hit it." You take a shot. Of course, you miss because archery is challenging. You don't just pick it up one day and become Robin Hood.

This time, your instructor doesn't give you a lot of corrective feedback, though. Instead, the teacher gives you a little bit of reassurance and encouragement. "Yeah, archery is hard. Keep trying." This time, things are different. You're still missing the target, but the corrections are coming from *you*. Because you can see the target clearly, you can also see where you're hitting in relation to that target (or defined learning goal). Your instructor is still there to offer some timely feedback when needed, but you are doing the lion's share of the work.

Eventually you manage to hit the target. Whose accomplishment is it this time? Yes, it's yours, because you are the one who performed the cognition and made adjustments to move closer to and eventually hit the target—what you're actually trying to do! This time, your instructor doesn't overpraise. Instead, the teacher just notices, and says something like, "Nice work. I knew you could do it," followed up with, "But don't get too excited. The goal is not to hit the target once and then promptly forget what was on the test. The goal is for you to become a proficient archer. Archery is a skill you will need to contend in the world. This skill matters! So keep shooting."

You keep shooting and over time, you become more and more proficient. Now your instructor introduces *rigor* and *novelty* by moving the target farther back, changing the point of aim or introducing variables, such as wind. The work becomes weirdly fun and even fulfilling. Motivation actually goes up, precisely because the skill is hard, and it's a challenge to *try* to get better. And, when you *try* to hit what you can see and continue to make progress, there's also a powerful motivating physiological response in the form of a *dopamine* release (Huberman, 2021). More about dopamine later, but just know all students, even your hard-core, tough-to-motivate students, are hardwired to seek experiences of progress.

Both archery learning scenarios look similar to the untrained eye; lots of aiming, missing, and trying again. However, the experiences and subsequent stories are fundamentally different. In the second scenario, you can see what you're aiming at! As a learner, you now have a *purpose*: to become a proficient archer. Your purpose isn't to simply comply with your teacher until you happen to get lucky and hit a target you can't really see. You know what the overall goal is, and you know what it looks like when you achieve it. Archery is a rigorous skill and difficult to learn, so you're going to miss the target a lot. But because you can see where you hit in relation to the target, you are empowered to adjust your aim and—given the chance—try again. You might get a little feedback from your teacher when it's most needed, and then you try again. *This* is called *learning*.

It takes a challenge worthy of a hero's effort to become a hero. Repeated attempts and failures are part of the learning process. You still might need some tips and coaching to become more reliable in your performance or as the task becomes more rigorous (such as when the teacher moves the target farther away or you are put in new or novel situations).

> *It takes a challenge worthy of a hero's effort to become a hero. Repeated attempts and failures are part of the learning process.*

In the activities of both scenarios, compliance and empowerment look similar to the untrained eye. In both scenarios, the learner is shooting arrows with a bow, but the goal is completely different. If you're a learner empowered to own your learning, you're no longer simply doing what your teacher says. It's not your job to be strictly compliant with what the teacher says at all. Your job is to learn how to reliably hit the target; it's to learn what it is you're supposed to learn, because you need to.

The experience of each scenario conditions the learner to take fundamentally different stances. In the first scenario, the stance is about *compliance*. You must submit and follow along. It feels like the activity is being *done to you*, like you're helpless, a victim, and untrusted in your capabilities, with no belief in your potential. In the second scenario, the stance is about *challenge*. The task is actually harder, but the learning journey is your own. It's not easy or comfortable to own the learning. Students often resist the responsibility at first. But ownership feels empowering, especially if it's acceptable to make mistakes. Because learners understand the goal, they have purpose. Because they have purpose, there is opportunity for profound reward. It's the stance of a hero, not a victim.

## Facilitating Learning, Rather Than Teaching

You can feel a noticeable difference in a classroom when you challenge students to own their learning. If learners can see the intended learning goal, and the teacher has helped students truly own it, they are empowered. Their demeanor changes; they move more and their shoulders are back. They're talkative, yet productive, and they're paying attention. They're willing to try and fail. They get frustrated with setbacks, but then seek feedback and make corrections.

During a visit to an underserved school in California, I worked with a team of teachers frustrated with the lack of motivation and ownership in their students. The team resisted my suggestions, believing somehow their students were too impoverished or too "low level" to take ownership. (This is not uncommon for team members stuck in their own fixed mindsets.) Finally, one of the teachers agreed to give a few of the strategies a try, particularly those helping students see the learning goals and self-assess. She sent me the following text message:

> Growth mindset is on my own mind. Revamped the progress tracker [a means for communicating learning goals] for the current unit . . . did it with all my classes today. Was fabulous! Students were engaged, pushing to better their own scores, working hard to use their resources, and showed improvement. I had students with better posture, smiles, and even dancing as they felt confident and proud of themselves. Eye-opening for many, including myself. (S. Nixon, personal communication, March 1, 2023)

However, in so many classrooms, that is not the scene. Often I see too much of teachers teaching and students compliantly sitting. Their eyes are dull, and they're disengaged. In many cases, these teachers are working extremely hard. They spend hours and hours designing lessons and activities. They work at unsustainable levels, often sacrificing their own family's well-being for their students. Teachers care so much! In many cases, they might even be really good at teaching and being really good deliverers, but that's not their job. A teachers' job is not to teach, but to ensure students *learn* what is intended (essential goals).

It sounds like I'm arguing semantics, but I'm not. This is a fundamentally different stance for teachers too. Who's doing most of the work in the first archery scenario? The teacher is; the teacher provides all the direction, correction, assessment, feedback, encouragement, and, honestly, most of the effort too. Consider when the teacher doesn't just have one archer, but many. It's exhausting and next to impossible when you have thirty would-be archers, all at different skill levels. When teachers (and not students) perform that much cognition, it's no wonder they go home exhausted and students go home ready to play.

Who's doing the lion's share of the work in the second scenario? The learner is! They are the ones working toward the goal because they can see it. Whose accomplishment is it when they become proficient? It's the learner's, because the teacher hasn't stolen it from them. Don't steal their struggle. If you steal their struggle, you steal their sense of accomplishment too.

> *Don't steal their struggle. If you steal their struggle, you steal their sense of accomplishment too.*

Obviously, archery isn't an essential skill for today's learners, but at one point it was for certain groups of people. If you weren't proficient, you didn't eat, regardless of how compliant you were. Here are some questions that prompt you to shift your thinking from a focus on teaching to a focus on learning and the development of the learner: What if your students only got to eat if they truly became proficiently skilled at what they were supposed to learn? Not just pass a test or hit the target once, but become proficient at reading, writing, solving problems, critically thinking, synthesizing texts to make viable claims, argumentation, collaborating, and so on. Would your practice change? Perhaps you are one of the rare teachers who already takes a truly learning-centered stance. But I would contend if most teachers really thought about it, they would spend a lot less time "teaching" if the stakes were so high. If that were the case, teachers would spend more time illuminating and communicating the intended learning goal, and less time having students take shots in the dark. They would be figuring out how to assess to diagnose specific deficits, and not just rank or sort students by *As*, *Bs*, *Cs* or other performance levels. Teachers would intervene based on those specific deficits. They would spend less time in front of the class and more time sitting side by side with students, empowering them and guiding them toward the goal.

In their book *Leaders of Learning*, researchers and coauthors Richard DuFour and Robert J. Marzano (2011) not-so-subtly imply the need for a shift in stance so district-level leaders, teachers, and everyone in between are all leaders of learning. If I could wave my magic wand, teachers would no longer be called *teachers*. *Leaders of learners*, *learning facilitators*, and *guides on the side* all seem more appropriate. Even better, what if teachers could use the experiences of learning skills (archery or anything else) as an intentional way to help students learn how to be in charge of their development as learners, and develop the grit, perseverance, and courage they need to achieve, along with improved metacognition and self-awareness? Could teachers use the learning of skills as a means for helping students see how powerful they really are? In other words, could educators help learners each truly become their own hero in their own story about their own learning journey? They would not only be learning-centric but also *learner*-centric—the ultimate goal being the development of the learners themselves. If this were the case, the title teachers could boldly claim for themselves would be nothing less than *hero makers*. The following sections illustrate some ways educators can ensure they are communicating the learning goal effectively.

Hattie (2009) explains, "Achievement is enhanced to the degree that students and teachers set and communicate appropriate, specific, and challenging goals" (p. 16). What is particularly interesting about this declaration is the notion that the level of achievement is commensurate to the degree of communication. So the more clearly you communicate the learning goals, the more students learn. Communication takes place through conversation, not presentation. The roots of the word *conversation* make the point. *Con-* means "with." *Vertere* means "to turn" something over (Conversation, n.d.). So, *conversation* means to turn something over together. To empower learners, teachers must, *with students*, repeatedly "turn it over." This kind of communication goes beyond just presenting the learning objective on the board.

## Models of Proficiency

So, how do you *communicate* the learning goal with clarity? There are many ways, but I find one method the most powerful in illuminating and communicating the learning goal, especially more rigorous and complex goals (such as writing, problem solving, critical thinking, interpreting a data set, performing music, art techniques, welding, and so on). The method involves the use of models. If you were to make one change in this area, make this one! Models of proficient student work are better than any success criteria, scale, or rubric for communicating to students what the learning is supposed to look like. By talking about the goal while also showing them actual examples of what proficient work might look like, learners start to see more clearly. Communication takes place. Good teachers point out what the models do or don't do to make them proficient examples. Piece by piece, the models demystify what students are aiming at and, as a result, learners can see the goal. In chapter 7 (page 105), you'll learn the nuts and bolts of how to create models, as well as other tools you will need to use the Hero-Maker

Framework to its fullest potential. For now, it's important to get a deeper understanding of how important models are to empowering students with clear learning goals.

Here are some ways you can share and discuss models of proficiency in your classroom.

» Explain why a particular skill matters or why it is an important skill for students and their future, not just "the test." Explain to learners why this is a skill they will need to compete in the world, why it *matters*.

» Use questions to help students understand the finer points. Ask students to ask a question of a partner. Ask them to explain the goal to a partner. Ask them to ask you questions. Simply listen to what they think the goal is and what the destination looks like when they get there. Ask them to draw a picture of what proficiency in the skill looks like. Do students understand what they're really aiming at?

» Talk about proficiency models every day. With so much consistent and intentional effort to keep the goal at the forefront of their gaze, students will see it.

» Cocreate new models together in class and discuss why certain work is proficient and other work is not quite. Discuss why some work is beyond proficiency or at an advanced level.

» Ask for students' intentional effort. "Will you help me? Will you do your part to learn this important skill?" By explaining why this skill matters and asking for their help, you're asking learners for intentional effort. More students will learn at deeper levels simply because they are now intentionally trying.

Sometimes when learning goals are more discrete, especially in the lower grades (like learning letter sounds or mathematics facts), models may not make as much sense to constantly refer back to. Use models where they make sense, but regardless, keep talking about the learning goal and keep it in the forefront of learners' gaze.

Performance-based classes like music will have recordings of certain sections of music students are learning they can listen to and compare their performance against. Teachers leading welding, coding, woodshop, physical education, and culinary classes likely already use models to demystify what kids are aiming at. With regard to essential skills of Mathematical Practices or some science critical competencies (like critical thinking and problem solving), video models make the most sense for showing students how to use certain steps to think through a problem. Video models are useful for learning speaking and listening skills, job interview skills, drama, performing medical procedures, and any other skill that someone observes to assess.

Communicating learning goals with students is an essential part of helping them take ownership of their own learning (Stiggins, 2008). Through your conversations with one another, you'll start to bring clarity to the destination students are heading toward (or the target they're aiming at).

## Clarity Brings Hope

Improved academic learning is important, but communicating the learning goal serves a more important purpose than just helping students learn essential academic skills. You're doing something much deeper here: you're giving *purpose* to journeyers. When students can see the destination—even if it's on a subconscious level—each step they take is bringing them closer to their goal. Learners know there is purpose in their effort (which gives them meaning), and meaning is a fundamental human need (Frankl, 2006; original work published 1946). Slowly, over time, you'll see that when students find purpose and meaning in their learning, the wellsprings of hope begin to slowly rise. Where hope is present, motivation is no longer a limiting factor.

Hope for a better world beckons all would-be journeyers. It's the call to adventure that Campbell (1949) clarifies, the effort to emulate archetypes that Jung (1954) describes, and the need for self-actualization that Maslow (1943) explains. For some students, seeing a learning goal they actually aim at is the beginning of that hope.

# The Power of Communication and Clarity

When I was a brand-new teacher at a high school in my home state of Nevada, as the newest member of the English department, I was assigned to teach a Tier 3 remediation class called *English Success*. This class was the last-ditch effort for students who had not yet passed the state writing proficiency exam. If they didn't pass the exam, they didn't graduate: no exceptions. My class of high school seniors had already taken the assessment multiple times and failed. Most would call these students a *rough crew* or worse. I did my best; I really did! I stressed and fretted over this class of a dozen students more than any of my other classes because I knew what was at stake. I knew if these students did not graduate from high school, the potential impact on their lives would be profound.

I would wake up in the middle of the night with what I call the *teacher dreams*— nightmares, really. Someone with more experience should have been teaching this class, but that was the culture of the school at the time. The message was clear: "Pay your dues, rookie!" I was the rookie and no one else wanted to teach it, even though there were teachers with far better skills. I did all the things I thought were beneficial. I tried to build relationships. I encouraged students, and was constantly looking for high-interest texts for them to read and write about. I gave them as much feedback as I could. I brought donuts. Decades later, I still remember their names.

In retrospect, when I think about that class, I know now they had their metaphorical blindfolds on. They couldn't see the target. They had years' worth of evidence to support their self-limiting stories, so even if they had wanted to work hard after years of conditioned apathy, they didn't know where to point their efforts. There was no clarity for them, and honestly, I didn't know what the state expected either. As a learner in their shoes, how do you motivate yourself to take a step when you don't know which direction to even face, especially when so many failed attempts have depleted all your hope?

When the test results came out, the last chance for my English Success class students, only a handful of them passed. Those who didn't, didn't get to walk across that graduation stage. It tore me up! The system had failed them. Worse, I had failed them.

Right before summer break, the state issued an invitation to any interested English teachers to attend a training where they would be trained as a scorer for the state writing proficiency exam. The closest session was a three-hour drive each way. It was on a Saturday, and you had to pay your own way to get there. But, if you became a certified scorer, you could go back a few months later, on another Saturday, and make two hundred dollars to sit for about ten hours and score papers. There was no way on this beautiful green earth I was going to go back and score papers for two hundred dollars! But I went to the training.

The training looked like this: a no-nonsense guy began with no preamble, just slapped down a sample of writing in front of about fifty of us, and said, "Use the rubric and score this." We did. The rubric was on a six-point scale. Sure, all of us were certified English teachers, so you'd think we'd know quality when we see it, especially with a rubric, right? Our scores were all over the place. Some teachers said the writing sample was a 6 while others said it was a 1, with everything in between.

We were all confident in our scores until we started to compare. UCLA emeritus professor and former teacher W. James Popham (2018) confirms our experience, noting the subjectivity embedded in grading, including bias and personal judgments, interpretation of the grading criteria, and inconsistency of evaluation. So much variance encourages students to engage in hoop-jumping compliance for this or that teacher, instead of focusing on actually getting better. The instructor explained that the essay was a 4 and then, using the rubric, he explained why.

The instructor then gave us another sample to score and asked, "What do you think it [the score] is?" We guessed, but tentatively this time. Using the rubric, the instructor explained the score and why. We did this repeatedly—about twelve or thirteen times over the course of the day. By the end of the day, this large group of people had achieved *inter-rater reliability*. Meaning, if I scored the essay a 3, you would also score it as a 3 or maybe a 4. Within one point was an acceptable range of variability. The target (or destination) became clear! I knew with clarity and confidence what I expected my students to learn and what it looked like when they learned it.

Interestingly—and in line with many of my college classes, where my professors held what was going to be on the test as top secret—the state also believed in secrecy. I still remember vividly, at the top of all of those sample papers the instructor used, written in big bold letters: *Not for instructional use. Do not share samples with students.* Even as such a young teacher that struck me as wrong! I thought, *if something is so important to learn that you will deleteriously impact students' lives if they don't learn it, don't you think you are obligated to let the learners know what it looks like when they've learned it? What do you mean I can't share these?* It didn't make sense to me then, and such practices of secrecy don't make sense to me now.

So, with righteous and youthful indignation, what do you think was the first thing I did in August when my new English Success class showed up? I didn't even hesitate; I shared those models with students every day. We spent the first six weeks of the school year doing little else. We got crystal clear by *communicating* what the intended learning goals were and in so doing, demystified the expectation for proficiency. We illuminated the target together. We didn't just do practice tests all year. We used the samples to better understand the components of good writing and practiced those components in authentic ways. Some might still argue I was teaching to the test. OK, if teaching to the test means *I clarified the elements of what I expected students to be able to do to be considered a proficient writer, gave feedback, and then had them practice the components they were weak in*, then I'm OK with the accusation. Helping learners understand what proficiency actually looks like isn't teaching to the test. It's good practice.

Armed with what author and educational consultant Michael Fullan (2003) calls "moral purpose" (p. 6), I remember spending nearly all three hours of the drive home from that training preparing my speech for when someone from the state might happen to walk into my classroom and see me violate the samples' official-looking directions for secrecy. I felt real fear that my choice could have consequences for me and my family. I thought maybe I could lose my job. But in that three-hour ride home, I concluded that what the system was doing was wrong. In fact, it was unconscionable that the state could create a requirement with such high stakes and then not clarify what that requirement actually looks like. It was poor educational practice, but more than that, I felt it was morally wrong and simply unfair. I refused to be complicit. So, in what felt like an act of civil disobedience, I shared the samples with students.

What I didn't understand then (but did years later) was no one person or group of people was trying to do wrong by students. The secrecy demand was just a vestige of an old system and old paradigms about sorting and selecting students—plenty of which still exists, and which educators need to conscientiously object to. In retrospect, my choice to clarify the learning expectations for students was an act that carried a lot less risk than I'd assumed. As someone who later ended up working for the same state-sponsored organization to provide trainings, I can imagine if that same gentleman who facilitated the training (or anyone else for that matter) had walked into my classroom and seen I was using those samples in class, he would have simply given me a thumbs-up, said, "Good teaching" and then walked away, no doubt promptly forgetting me and the experience.

After administering the last test that following year, I was as anxious as my English Success students for their results. On the morning the results came, one of my learners came bursting into my room with the results held high in her hand, smiling from ear to ear. Nearly tackling me in a hug, she laughed and cried with pure ecstatic joy, exclaiming, "I passed! I passed!" We then laughed and cried together.

This student was an exceptional athlete and this was the last step she needed. She had multiple scholarship offers for track and basketball. For her, the opportunity to go to college would break generational curses of victimization, abuse, and poverty. Not only would she have a chance to be the hero in her own story but also create a turning point in her family's history. She battled that test like it was a fierce dragon even though she failed in her first attempts. She got knocked down in the dirt, but continued to get back up and try again, persevering toward a target she could finally see. She was and is nothing less than a hero! She already knew how to work hard from her experience on the field and in the gym. She just hadn't been able to see the target or destination in her English classes.

Three times the number of my English Success students passed that year, compared to the first year. What's interesting is that truly little changed. My *teaching* wasn't any different, and my pedagogy really didn't change. My strategies didn't change. In fact, we read the same texts and did mostly the same assignments. The only difference in getting dramatically better results was that I began clarifying the overarching intended learning goals in crystal-clear terms. Students could see it, so they knew what they were aiming at. They knew what the destination looked like and where they were going. I simply illuminated the destination by using the models to clearly communicate it.

You may feel like you're committing an act of civil disobedience when you start making decisions about your curriculum to focus on those most essential items. You may feel nervous as you redefine your criteria of success to include the development of self-efficacy as your primary purpose. You may feel like there is a risk of students missing something that "will be on the test" if you don't cover all the standards and curricular minutiae. Be brave! Surround yourself with a supportive team and make your choices together. Nothing about deciding what is absolutely essential within your curriculum is wrong. It's the right thing to do, despite directions in bold letters from for-profit programs or other sources. Educators must narrow down which skills really matter and are worth learning at deep rigorous levels, especially if they are going to use rigorous learning to intentionally develop student self-efficacy.

## Concluding Thoughts

One of the roles of a wizard or hero maker is to help cut through the chaos and illuminate the path toward a worthwhile destination and meaningful purpose. Students must know their purpose is learning essential academic skills, but they also must understand they are learning these skills for the even greater purpose of developing into powerful individuals, ready to claim their space and contend in a world that won't hand them anything! They are on a journey to learn skills and transform themselves. Teachers need to embrace their true role of guiding students and illuminating the destination on their journey to learning and self-transformation. It all starts with communicating the learning goals.

Powerful teachers are crystal clear about what they want students to learn. They know the end destination with clarity, and they want nothing more than to get their students there. Each teacher's style and pedagogy will vary greatly. I've seen the charismatic types of the world who stand on tables prompting chants, raps, and cheers, and use dynamic cooperative learning experiences. I've also seen the old-school teacher before rows of desks, primarily lecturing but engaging every student, their eyes glued on her, and her adapting, changing, giving feedback, and ensuring every single one of her students is proficient. It's not about pedagogy, style, or strategy—it's about *intentionality*. These powerful teachers will do what it takes to get their students to the destination. The destination is what matters, not the path.

> *It is through the struggle that heroes become strong.*

However, there are teachers even beyond these powerful learning-focused teachers. Next-level teachers intentionally focus on ensuring their students learn the essentials, but that's not the only goal. They understand that the real goal is transformation of the learner. These master teachers focus on learning as a means for helping the learner develop into a powerful individual, ready to face the world. This level of master not only gets good academic results but also changes the trajectory of lives. These teachers are wizards. They're hero makers.

Keep reading. The next chapters explain how to continue illuminating the path of empowerment without stealing the struggle of the journey from learners. For it is through the struggle that heroes become strong.

CHAPTER 2

# Leverage Relationships of Trust to Help Students Overcome Fear

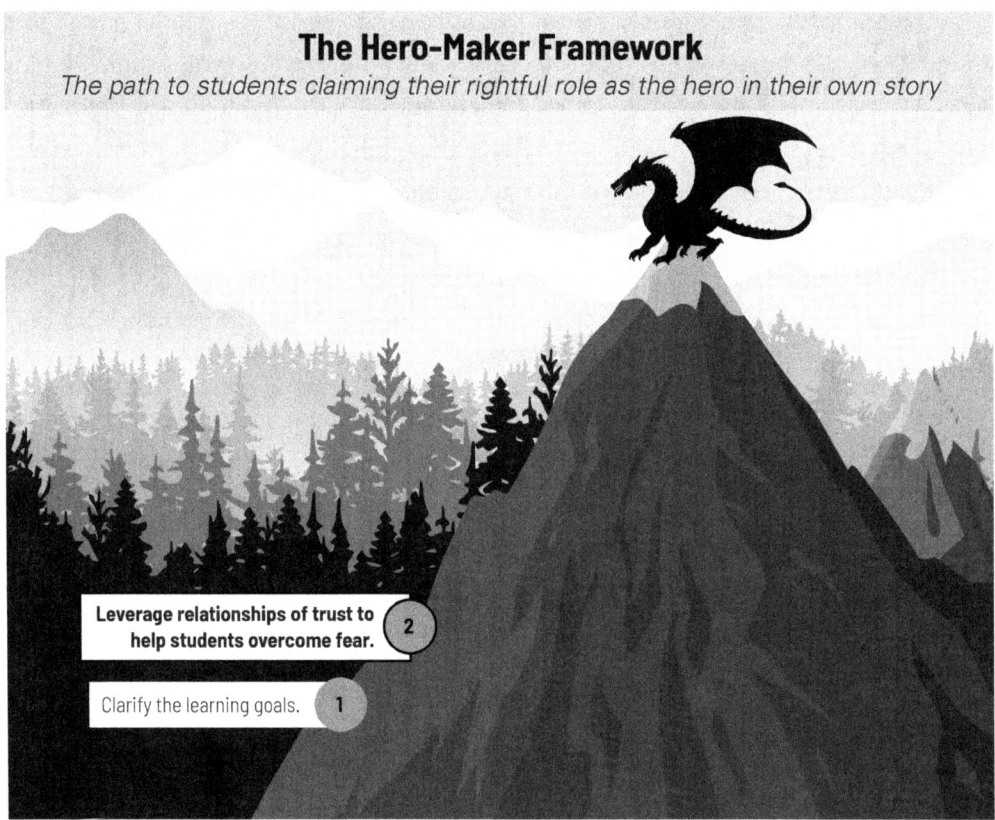

I've been to a lot of schools. I've never heard anyone say, "Oh yeah, relationships? They're not very important. We don't really do that around here." Most everyone understands relationships in a school, class, or team are important! Relationships provide safety, a caring voice, and someone to listen and turn to when problems arise. Learners are more motivated and learning increases when relationships are present (McKay & Macomber, 2023). However, to empower students to become heroes on their own their learning journey, a certain kind of relationship is needed.

Describing *the hero's journey*, Campbell (1949) explains that the presence of a mentor in every hero's story is important to a learner's development. The mentor is often a wise elder who may help learners on their hero's journey in a number of ways. The mentor may help heroes hear the call to adventure or give them tools to get started on their journey. Mentors provide training, advice, wisdom, and encouragement, usually at a critical moment when the hero needs it most. The pattern of a mentor is obvious in some of the most popular stories of all time, such as *The Lord of the Rings*, the Harry Potter series, *The Chronicles of Narnia*, and stories about King Arthur. In each of these works, the wise sage is nothing less than a wizard!

All would-be heroes need a wizard in their corner, but what is a wizard? A *wizard* is wise and powerful, so powerful that when a wizard says something will happen, it happens. It's almost as if the wizard can predict the future. (Can't you almost predict the future for some of your students, especially if they don't change the path they're on?) While wizards are highly competent (and not to be trifled with), they are also kind and generous toward the hero, and see goodness and potential in the hero. Wizards provide support when it's really needed, but they don't steal the journey, struggle, or decisions from the hero. They help prepare the hero to face inevitable challenges. Their wisdom often comes from having faced similar challenges themselves.

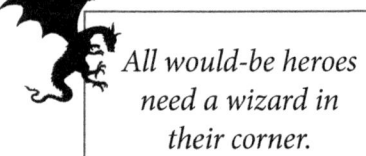

*All would-be heroes need a wizard in their corner.*

Because of their competence and integrity, the wizard's words are particularly powerful. If the wizard says something, others trust it as the truth. If they believe in a hero's potential, that potential is real. Probably most important to the would-be heroes are the words of encouragement the wizard offers when they need it most, right at the moment when heroes are doubting their ability to face fears. Interestingly, the word *encourage* literally means "to put courage into" someone (Encourage, n.d.). Because of earned competence and trustworthiness, the wizards' words of encouragement are believable and almost magical, helping the heroes believe they can take a step toward the darkness of their fears.

There is no difference between a hero and a learner. A *hero* is a learner, and to your learners—believe it or not—you are a *wizard* (or at least you have an opportunity to be). Translating the image of a wizard beyond Campbell's (1949) mythological dialect, a *wizard* is simply a teacher or mentor who builds a positive relationship with students and *uses* those relationships to empower students to step into their rightful role as heroes. A mentor acts with integrity, never breaking that trust, but leveraging it to help their students answer the call to journey on a productive path toward ownership and empowerment. Mentors do this by helping students change their story and begin to see themselves as capable heroes in their own story.

As I discuss in the introduction (page 1), students need new experiences of success on which to base their new story. To help them experience that success, a first step is often helping students just find enough motivation or courage to actually *try*. A relationship of trust with a credible and competent adult can be the key for unlocking effort, if the adult knows how. Before I explain how, you need to understand why kids need courage in the first place, and what's keeping them from really trying, sometimes even when they can see what they're aiming at.

# Fixed Mindset and Fear

Cody had a fixed mindset in the introduction (page 5). He had attached his entire identity to failure. It wasn't just that he had failed a lot in the past, it was that he believed *he* was a failure. Cody conflated his past performance with his current identity, a common misperception among many (young and old), regardless of where they are on the achievement continuum. Cody believed, like so many, that his identity was the story he was telling himself about himself. And that story was so strong it was virtually guaranteed to come to fruition. Weirdly, there is safety in the predictability of failure.

> *There is safety in the predictability of failure.*

Like all people stuck in a fixed mindset, Cody had potential for something much more than his current story. But if you've come to a story through experience, others cannot really pep-talk you into a new story. You must have new experiences of actual success. The problem is, effort in the face of failure, actually putting yourself out there and *trying*, can be terrifying. The following sections detail some common factors that contribute to fear and hinder effort and perseverance.

## Fear of Failure

If the subconscious mind could talk, it might reason something like, "If I actually try, I risk feeling like a failure, which I've experienced enough times to know it hurts. I don't want to hurt or be vulnerable. If I choose not to try and I fail, at least it was my choice." In addition, the pain of repeated failure can develop into emotional trauma, which intensifies the self-limiting inner-critic's story. All of this can start to shape one's identity. Author Echart Tolle (2016) explains that identity is generally developed through identification with "form," which consists of things such as material possessions, perceptions, and especially experiences. He elucidates:

> The word *identification* is derived from the Latin word *idem*, meaning "same", and *facere* which means "to make." So when I identify with something (or an experience), I "make it the same." The same as what? The same as I. (Tolle, 2016, p. 35)

The *ego* is the part of people's subconscious mind largely responsible for these identifications and, therefore, people's identity development and protection (Ego, n.d.). A threat to identity, metaphysical as it may be, can literally feel as scary as a physical threat. When a student's ego is in protective mode, that student will avoid unfamiliar situations where the outcome is uncertain. If you have experienced a lot of failures without overcoming those failures, it's likely your ego is going to step in to protect you from having similar experiences. When teachers ask learners to try, after they've failed over and over again, their self-defeating story and egoic reactions just get stronger—without some help to disrupt the cycle.

Oddly, fear can also take over when learners' fixed mindsets tell them they are capable. "Fear of failure often stems from perfectionism. When people have extremely high standards, it often seems like nothing lives up to their expectations. This includes their own performance and achievements." (Cherry, 2023). Have you had students whose self-image was positive, yet they resisted taking risks? They don't like ambiguous directions and become like Velcro, asking for directions and validation, "Am I doing it right?" Their parents, teachers, and peers have told them for years they're "smart," and their good grades are evidence of this. They develop a positive—but fixed—mindset. These students are happy to continue trying when it's a task they know they can succeed at, but resist venturing out of their comfort zone for fear they'll fail, and thus put a crack in their "I'm smart" story and identity.

## Fear of Rejection

This fear of failure plays into the deep-seated fear of rejection. Pioneer researchers in the area of belonging, professors Roy F. Baumeister and Mark R. Leary (1995), write extensively on humans' natural and strong need to belong as a fundamental human motivation (also see Allen, Gray, Baumeister, & Leary, 2022). The reason is because "humans are deeply dependent on their group membership," and it's within group membership that people learn how to "survive" (Over, 2016). Looking like you don't know what you're doing in front of your peers can feel like you're losing your "ticket to survival" at some level. This is why many adults list their fear of public speaking as worse than their fear of death (Croston, 2012). In the subconscious mind, egoic fear can grip a learner, thus saying something "stupid" will lead to losing acceptance from the group (and imminent death). That's not true of course, but this is how powerful potential failure can *feel*.

Part of the overall problem here is many students perceive failure not as a description of their current performance level, but as a description of their inherent abilities. Learners need to understand that failing is part of learning and is not permanent. To bring your practices into alignment with this understanding means you must be careful with how you communicate things like grades too. Grades should be a fluid depiction of a learner's current position on the learning continuum in relation to a defined learning goal, not a permanent judgment.

## The Stress Response

In moments of *stress*, people's unconscious mind can't tell the difference between an existential threat to their identity or an actual life-threatening threat. An *acute stress response* is activated in an ancient part of the brain designed to help avoid saber-toothed tigers. In the moment of an acute stress response, the amygdala dumps powerful stress hormones like adrenaline and epinephrine through the body (Guy-Evans, 2023). The classic behavioral translation to moments of felt stress, depending on the situation, is often fight, flight or freeze (Guy-Evans, 2023). While most people are aware of these classic responses, there is a fourth *F*: *fawning* means acting in a way to please someone in power to avoid conflict (Guy-Evans, 2023). In school, this manifests as students doing just enough to get by so their teachers, parents, or coaches will stay off their back (if they are lucky enough to have these adults in their lives). Even though students might be getting by, they are not taking the active stance of a learner or hero. Another response to the stress of potential failure is simply avoidance.

For a lot of learners, it's easier to just not try, so they quit before they start: you hear statements like "I can't do that," "I'm no good at that," and "That's too hard." While some kids with perfectionistic tendencies might frantically chase points, grades, and praise to validate their story (or their depiction of their identity), those same seemingly capable kids have such strong egos they will also *avoid* potential identity attacks by never putting themselves in the risky situation of accepting a stretch challenge. And if they do find themselves in a situation where they might actually fail, they will often quit before even trying.

Clearly, fawning and avoidance are not behaviors exclusive to students like Cody. If you really pay attention, you'll notice many learners are struggling to reach their potential because of fear. Fear is what keeps people of all ages and levels of achievement from leaning into real challenges; fear keeps them playing it "safe." Fear is the single greatest obstacle to people realizing their potential—even you!

## How to Help Students Face Their Fears

If fear is such an incredibly powerful force that keeps learners stuck, how do educators help them start to release its grip? The answer is disarmingly simple—*students must face their fear!* And *teachers* (with their wizard-like skills) must help students face that fear.

Generally speaking, and in true Jungian fashion, facing fears is the only way to really overcome them on the way to becoming who you can be (Jung, 1954). What would bene-fit you the most lies on the other side of the thing you fear the most. Students must face their fear to move toward their potential and assume the role of hero.

> *What would benefit you the most lies on the other side of the thing you fear the most.*

Campbell (1949) explains, archetypically, this idea of realizing potential is represented in stories in the exact moment when the hero decides to face a dragon, and then does face it. Don't overlook the importance of the image of a dragon. When you really think about it, a dragon is terrifying! Imagine facing a giant snake that flies, breaths fire, has nearly impenetrable skin, and is highly intelligent. Scary, right? However, Campbell (1949) writes on the other side of this terrifying, fire-breathing serpent lies a thing of tremendous value, such as gold. The reward makes it worth facing the dragon. But invariably, the hero's reward is more than just gold; the hero becomes something more by facing the dragon. As learners face more and more such challenges, they undergo a transformation, which is the true reward. They become more confident in facing future challenges, precisely because of the experience of facing challenges in the past. Even if they might fail on first attempts, they try again, metaphorically getting up after being knocked down in the dirt. This is the role of a hero. This is also a learner.

For so many students, and perhaps many educators, fear of failure or rejection is the dragon lurking in the darkness. It's scary to face it and be vulnerable, even if you see the potential benefit to you and the people you love. The fear can be paralyzing. This is when you need a guide or mentor to help you find some courage. The following sections translate these concepts to the classroom, and explore the importance of relationships of trust and how you can leverage those relationships to help students face their fears.

## The Importance of Trust

Carl R. Rogers (1951), an American psychologist known for his person-centered psychotherapy, believed that a supportive relationship is an essential key for learners to align and strive toward their potential, pursue their goals, and live a fulfilling life. Psychologist Albert Bandura (1997) claimed that the same type of supportive relationship can be a powerful contributor to the development of an individual's sense of self-efficacy. Relationships with adults in particular are key to students' development of motivation and resilience, and the ability to overcome obstacles and achieve goals. Learners operating out of fear will take a tentative step toward their potential, even in the face of dragon-like fears, *if* they trust you, and you encourage them. An example might be a learner who doesn't usually engage in physical education class starting to do pushups because he has begun to trust the encouragement and confidence of his teacher. It might be a learner who struggles to speak in front of her peers being willing to be a project team leader because she trusts her teacher, and her teacher told her she is ready for the challenge.

It isn't about whether the learner likes the teacher or doesn't; it's about *trust*. Students must learn that when the teacher says something is going to happen, it happens—especially if the teacher puts a task in front of a student and says they can do it. If you say students can do a thing, you better make sure they do, even if it takes multiple attempts. If you set a consequence or reward for a behavior, and the behavior occurs, administer the consequence or give the reward. You must have integrity and keep your word. You don't have to have all the answers. If you don't know something, say you don't. If you make a mistake, own it, and apologize. Just be consistent and honest, because if you are—and show you have students' interests at heart—over time, learners will trust you, and believe what you say. Then, when you place an appropriate challenge in front of them and tell them, "You know you can do it!" they will believe *you*, even when they don't believe themselves.

> *Learners operating out of fear will take a tentative step toward their potential, even in the face of dragon-like fears, if they trust you, and you encourage them.*

Child psychiatrist and school design expert Pamela Cantor (2018) explains why, from a biological perspective, a relationship of trust allows students to take a step. When adversity occurs, the brain releases the stress hormone *cortisol*, which produces negative effects on the learning center of the brain called the *limbic system*. A consistent relationship of trust provides a buffering and can be used to challenge learners to take a step toward learning. If students have a buffering relationship and the (accompanying) release of the hormone oxytocin, this will oppose many of the negative effects of cortisol and result in some of the resilience we see and return to a normalization of brain architecture (Cantor, 2018).

When students try or take a risk in this situation, ensure they are successful! This is an important point you can't overlook. If you promise a student they can take a step, you need to make sure they do, especially at first. If they need scaffolding or other support, provide it. Otherwise, the student may not trust you the next time you ask. If they try and fail, or require too much help from you, you have only reinforced their old narrative. Students don't have to conquer their dragon all at once, you just need to ensure whatever step they attempt to take, they are successful. The following section tells a story that illustrates this.

## A Story About Eddie

On a family trip, two of my sons and I stumbled on a park with a gigantic old slide. It's the kind of slide built long before people thought about liability. It had three different sections of descents made of thigh-scorching metal, at least seventy-five feet long, and steep! My oldest son (who was ten at the time) said, "Cool!" and went right to the top. Down he flew, no hesitation.

I looked at my youngest son, Eddie (who was six at the time) and asked, "Do you want to go down that slide?"

He stared me down defiantly with wide eyes and said, "Nope. Too scary!"

Taking seriously my fatherly role to encourage my children to take acceptable risks, I encouraged, "Come on, Eddie. It'll be fun." (I knew it was acceptably safe because his brother didn't die.)

"No way!" was his response.

Eddie is the youngest in our family, so he has the benefit of a more experienced father than his older siblings. As a younger father, I probably would have scooped him up, taken him right to the top, said "Have fun!" as I gave him a nudge down the slide. But what would that have done to our relationship? It would have eroded trust and potentially traumatized him. It likely would have exacerbated the fear, which he would carry forward from that point on. So what did I do? I decided I wasn't going to give up. I knew Eddie would find something of value at the bottom of that slide, exactly because he would have to face his fear to get there.

I nodded my understanding, and said "OK, I get that it's scary. I hear you. It's really tall." I let the validation sit for a moment, then I tried again. "I get that you don't want to do the whole thing, but do you think you could go down just the bottom section? That's no taller than the slide we have in the park by our house." While he looked at the bottom section, I went on, "I'll hold you up there until you tell me you're ready to go. I promise."

He agreed to take the step because he trusted me to do what I said. I hoisted him up on the bottom section of the slide, which was about fifteen feet tall and fairly steep. I held his little legs and asked, "Are you ready?" He nodded. I double checked, "Are you sure? Do want me to let go?"

He nodded again and said, "I'm ready. Let go." I let go and he glided unscathed to the bottom.

As he climbed back up the stairs toward me, I asked him, "What did you think? Want to do it again?"

This time he went down from the same place without help. He did that a couple more times. I asked casually, "What's next?" He climbed a little higher the next time and a little higher on each trip down the slide, starting to feel the rush of the slide (and the dopamine and adrenaline boost) from succeeding at something a little scary.

Eyeballing the ladder, finally Eddie climbed carefully all the way up. I took video of him on my phone as he prepared to let go at the top, a thing that, just a few minutes earlier, he said was "too scary." The fear was evident on his face the moment right before he let go. But so was the determination. He let go and slid like a dream, wind blowing his fluffy six-year-old hair all the way to the bottom of that transformational slide.

When he came to a stop, he stood on his feet, raised both fists in the air, jumped up and down and yelled with unabashed, dragon-slaying pride, "I did it! I did it!" I fought back tears, because I had just watched my son face his fear, transform just a bit, and realize a little more of his potential. It was just one experience, but it was a piece of evidence in a story where he is becoming a capable individual who knows he can face his fears—a dragon slayer.

I couldn't get Eddie off the slide after that. Even the bribe of going to find some ice cream wasn't enough to convince him. I engaged Eddie in a metacognitive conversation to help him realize what he had just done, and it became a reference point for facing other fears later. More on the role of metacognition in chapter 5 (page 79).

## The Zone of Proximal Development

Some students (like my eldest son) will climb right to the top of the slide or perform the tasks of the essential standard. And some students, like Eddie, are going to need some support or scaffolding as educators help them make it to the top. Make no mistake: the standard is the standard. The top of the slide is the top of the slide. I'm not talking about moving it, because what message would I send to learners if I moved the standard? "I don't believe in you." I would never do that to Eddie or anyone else! What I'm talking about is figuring out how to support students in getting there regardless of where they start.

A simple example for fifth-grade students learning the skill of citing text evidence might be providing sentence frames or starters. A teacher could provide students with graphic organizers like T-charts or story maps to help them organize their thoughts, identify evidence, and link the evidence to their interpretations or answers. The teacher might work closely with a small group of students whose needs are more intense as they learn the concepts of finding evidence and then begin to gradually release responsibility. Sometimes, just like with Eddie, it's simply a conversation about what steps learners can take and then asking, "What's next?" But only provide the scaffolded steps if students need them. My oldest son would have been annoyed and bored at my requirement of compliance if I had made him work his way to the top like Eddie. If students are ready to go all the way to the top of the slide (or ready to demonstrate proficiency in citing evidence), don't hold them back by making them follow scaffolds appropriate for others.

The way to bridge the gap between what students are currently able to do and what they can't do yet is to start with something they know they can do and gradually provide increasingly difficult tasks. Give them small wins along the way, until they reach the top. In other words, help students take progressive steps within their *zone of proximal development (ZPD)*.

The *ZPD* is a concept Lev S. Vygotsky (1986), known for his work on children's psychological development, describes as that sweet spot between what someone already knows how to do and what they don't yet know, or when the task is just beyond the learner's current capability. If a task is in the ZPD, it's a bit of a stretch, but with the right support, not such a big stretch that the learner can't do it. This is the sweet spot where small wins that lead to growth happen.

The ZPD is where a true wizard can really make a difference. Teachers can leverage their relationship capital to encourage learners to take an appropriate and manageable step toward new learning. To do this, you must know what the would-be hero's ZPD is. You need to determine the appropriate academic step and the learner's emotional readiness to face that step. Students will take a step into the darkness toward their potential commensurate with the level of trust they have in you. If they trust you a lot, they will take a big step. If they don't trust you very much or have been burned too many times in the past, they may only be willing to take a small step.

For example, when learning to add fractions with unlike denominators, some learners, after initial exposure and some practice, will be ready to go right to the metaphorical top of the slide and start solving problems. Some will need more practice, and some will need intervention. But it's important the intervention is within their ZPD. Some learners' ZPD might be to simply understand the concept of common denominators. To understand common denominators is their step or goal. Some students' ZPD might be to conceptualize what a fraction is. Part of your role is to know what their ZPD is, and to leverage your relationship of trust to help them to take an appropriate step and be successful. Then, you help them take another step. You haven't changed the overall expectation; you just help the heroes take incremental steps toward their final destination.

Slowly but repeatedly, facilitate new experiences and new evidence of success on which students craft their new story. Inherent to these ZPD conversations is a high level of competence in your assessment and feedback practices. I discuss both more deeply in chapter 4 (page 63).

## Reflection on Trusting Relationships

Teachers each approach developing relationships of trust differently. Following are some tips teachers can use to consider how to improve the quality of trust in relationships with their learners.

>> Notice things about your students—their likes, dislikes, talents, or other interests. Don't overpraise or label those things, just notice them, and communicate that you notice. This is a quick way to start developing trust.

>> Ask questions and practice empathy by validating when a student shares a concern, fear, or even a complaint. Don't discount the fear or story. For example, a simple, "I hear you" or, "Thank you for being honest" can go a long way. Feeling heard is a quick inroad toward trust.

>> Don't shy away from the hard conversations (age appropriate, of course). Be real with students. They will appreciate your integrity and honesty when you don't gloss over community, school, or world challenges. Share your own experiences, especially of your failures and the wisdom you gained from them. Your stories will communicate that you get it, care, and can be trusted.

>> Be consistent and transparent with routines, procedures, expectations, and commitments. If you say you're going to do something, follow

through. Wizards make exceptions only when wisdom dictates it is necessary. Otherwise, they are immoveable even in the face of pressure. Is there opportunity for you to be more consistent? If so, in what ways?

» Challenge students to take steps that stretch them. Provide the scaffolds they need, and then simply notice when they are successful. Without any surprise in your voice, you can point out you were right by saying, "I knew you could do it." Over time students' trust in your competence will grow, and when they hear you say, "I know you can do it," they will believe you.

» Consider the ways the wizards in your life impacted you. Take some time to journal about the impact they had on your development. Are there ways you could replicate those impacts?

## Concluding Thoughts

Eddie trusted me, and because of that trust, he was willing to take my guidance and accept a challenge within his ZPD. He was willing to be uncomfortable, but only incrementally and with encouragement. The same is true for many of your learners. They might not look or act like they're scared, but they are. They might look at the top (or the whole standard), but are too afraid to try. But if students trust you and you ask, they will take a step within their ZPD toward facing the dragon of their potential. The result: they will try! And trying is a necessary first step to trading in the old victim identity of a fixed mindset for a new hero identity in their story.

# CHAPTER 3

# Select Worthy Content to Help Students Develop Skills

**The Hero-Maker Framework**

*The path to students claiming their rightful role as the hero in their own story*

**Select worthy content to help students develop skills.** 3

Leverage relationships of trust to help students overcome fear. 2

Clarify the learning goals. 1

Content matters! However, it doesn't matter for the same reasons it used to. In the past, it was more important to *know* things. Now, you can look up just about any fact or piece of content knowledge in 2.2 seconds: "Hey, Siri!" With devices imbued with artificially intelligent connections to the world's knowledge in nearly everyone's hands, "knowing stuff" is growing far less important. Content knowledge alone is an antiquated goal. However, when teachers use content properly, it is still a powerful driver for helping students learn what they need.

Worthy content will engage students deeply, becoming a vehicle for their development of essential academic skills and personal dispositions, such as self-efficacy. *Worthy content*, a term former educator and best-selling author Mike Schmoker (2011) popularized, is content compelling enough to be worth truly engaging in the learning process. To invest the effort to critically think about something in depth, and then to read, write, and have deep discourse about it requires the content to matter. It might be a piece of literature with themes students can relate to. It might be a real-world problem in the community for students to solve using the scientific method or mathematics skills. It could be a song, piece of art, car-restoration project, social problem, or story about an animal, all depending on community context and age appropriateness. Worthy content is worth wrestling with because it matters and is relevant enough to learners that they will engage on a deep level.

However, the goal isn't to *learn the content*. Students learning the skills and dispositions through the struggle is the goal. With proper use of content, you can ignite varying degrees of a learner's passion. Skilled teachers will harness that passion to help students develop skills and dispositions that will serve them in the future—long past the relevancy of the current event, project, or discussion.

> *Potential heroes will step into their role to fight for what matters to them.*

Potential heroes will step into their role to fight for what matters to them. They will learn, transform themselves, and face dragons for things they are passionate about and that have purpose and meaning. They don't fight for things that don't matter to them. Why would they? In fact, you should expect they will likely fight *against* being made to do things that don't matter.

Students like Cody (see page 5) are among perhaps the most glaring examples of learners who need to change their story and find something to strive for. Consultant and coach Susan Scott (2004) asks, "What are you pretending not to know?" After Cody, I couldn't pretend not to know many other students were victims in their story, and for multiple reasons. The strategy for their story is to do just enough to get by, or enough to get the grade their parents or coaches are comfortable with. However, these learners are not really engaged or owners of their learning. Secondary teachers have always seen this story manifest in students' attitudes, but it's becoming more evident and more common; it's creeping down into the lower grades too (Brenneman, 2016; Willcoxon & Marken, 2023). Worthy content can inspire these learners.

# A Story About Jentri

Let me illustrate the importance of worthy content with another story. When the COVID-19 pandemic hit and my own children, like everyone else's, stayed home to do online school, it was a challenge. At the time, my youngest daughter, Jentri, was in the second grade. She is a bright-eyed student who climbs trees, catches bugs, reads above her grade level, and is inherently curious. School generally comes easily for her. With her school-issued laptop in hand, Jentri came to me, eyes clouded with frustration and welling up with tears, and said, "Dad, I don't know how to do this."

I recognized what she was working on. It was a computer-generated mathematics placement assessment. It's one of those tests that if you get the question right, the next question is a little harder. If you get the question wrong, the next one is a little easier. This test is designed to give teachers broad information about their students' level of understanding in mathematics. If teachers use such tools properly, they can be useful. Jentri had been at this assessment for over an hour, so I looked at the problem she was stuck on. It was about square roots! I laughed out loud and said, "Oh, Sweetie, you're not supposed to know how to do this! This is way above second grade."

I explained to her how the assessment worked. I told her, "Your teacher is going to use this to make online assignments based on where you're at in your learning." I explained she should just guess and get the question wrong. If she didn't, she'd end up doing square roots as a second grader!

Her bright eyes came back as she shared what she took away from our conversation as the main point: "You mean I'm going to get to do stuff above second grade?"

I said, "Well, yeah. You probably shouldn't be doing square roots, but yes, if you need work above the second-grade level to challenge you, that's what you'll get." Yes, I know! I'm in the future now too, and I realize it was a mistake to say that to her. I should have known teachers weren't going to have time to differentiate for different learners' needs during a pandemic; they were just trying to figure out how to do online school. I messed up!

Fast-forward to the following week. My kids were hammering away at their online work, sitting at the kitchen table in their pajamas with pancake-syrup sticky fingers. In less than an hour, Jentri was done, and asked if she could watch her favorite YouTube channel. I said, "You're done? Really? You're sure?" She glanced sideways, but nodded the affirmative. "Let's take a look." We pulled up her class dashboard and sure enough, she hadn't even touched her mathematics. I clicked into it, "You haven't even started your math yet." That bright cheery disposition turned cloudy again and she looked down as she mumbled something. "What is it?" I asked, ready to listen to what she said.

She looked up, tears now running, "This is stupid!"

I kneeled and tried to understand her frustration, "What do you mean, Sweetie?"

In a flurry she explained, pointing, "Do you see all these assignments?" She thundered on, "This is all kindergarten, maybe first-grade work. It's not even second-grade work, Dad! I already know how to do all this stuff!" There was a pause and then she concluded, "This is stupid!"

I didn't respond; I got it. She was only in second grade, so how could she articulate what she was feeling other than to cry and say it was "stupid"? But I knew what she meant. Jentri was being asked to do something that had no real value to her whatsoever, especially after I had set her up to believe she would receive work at her level of learning. In adult language, she felt like she was "jumping through hoops." She was compelled to do something simply for the sake of compliance. It was busywork, pure and simple, and Jentri knew it.

I thought about this situation from the teacher's perspective. Of course, the teacher didn't have time to look at my daughter's mathematics placement data. She was just scrambling to try to post tasks online so learners could keep "doing school." In part, I set my daughter up for this frustration the week before when I explained how the placement assessment *should* work. But underneath this situation is something bigger; it's an under-tow of disengagement related to forced compliance. *Compliance* perniciously undercuts motivation and pervades many educational practices, from assignments and grading to so-called interventions and beyond (Hansen, 2020).

Here was Jentri's dilemma: those assignments were strictly about compliance for her. Doing meaningless tasks you don't want to do doesn't feel good, *especially* when someone is compelling you to do them. So Jentri was stuck. She could do the many assignments strictly out of compliance, or she could risk damaging part of her identity in her story as a "good student" and disappointing her teacher. Her immediate reaction to the dissonance was to escape the current problem by diving into the world of thumbs-ups, subscribes, and clicks, where *she* controls her experience.

## Forced Compliance Creates Resistance

Students who have grown up with the internet are more powerful than any other generation in the world's history. This is because they've had artificially intelligent devices with access to the world's knowledge at their fingertips since they were young. Most of today's students learn to swipe a screen before they learn to turn a page.

Almost without exception, they have access to these devices and a World Wide Web of interconnected ideas, knowledge, entertainment, and even alternate realities. Therefore, students today have the ability to shape almost their entire experiential lives, down to the minute! They freely curate, choice by choice, the media they ingest, music they listen to, games they play, and constant connectivity with family, friends, and acquaintances. For many students, that digital world without borders is more real than the real world.

There's more. Not only are students empowered with instant choice as consumers of abundant content but also *all* are influencers of it too, every single one of them. Through choice after choice, students help cocreate their very perceptions of reality and future options of experiences. As an audience who participates, they tell creators what to create next through views, likes, and dislikes, subscribes and unsubscribes, shares, and the comments they post. Students don't just consume all that media and information, they *change* it, shaping the content as it's produced. Now celebrities interact with, respond to, and foster relationships with their audiences, creating entire online communities. In true democratic fashion, the most clicks win, telling content creators what to create more of, and each person's vote counts, including kids' votes. They are natives among all this technology and access, completely at home in this world. Students today think differently about the world and planet, and their equal place in it; they are powerful!

So is it any surprise when teachers demand compliance on tasks that don't have meaning or relevance, they get resistance from students? When teachers place students in conditions where teachers expect compliance—without choice or meaning—it feels archaic and even oppressive. In the absence of choice and meaning, when students can learn anything at any time, anywhere outside school, many feel formal education is obsolete. Many students feel victimized, like they are doing their culturally obligated time, a twelve-year act of compliance before they get out into the *real world*.

In classrooms without clear relevance or meaning (at least to learners), teachers hear things like, "This is stupid!" "I hate school," or "When will I ever use this?" When teachers compel students to do something, they're not in a position of empowerment. Students are definitely not in the role of a hero, like in their video game or online community. Compulsion is what people do *to* someone. In fact, the only likely way to be a hero when compulsion is involved is to resist the compulsion and rebel. When it feels like things are being done to learners, and they are powerless to do anything to change those conditions, that's akin to being the victim in their story. Teachers don't want students to be victims; they want students to be heroes! A key part of empowerment and ownership of learning is to provide content students can really care about.

## Purpose, Meaning, and Passion

> *Students have the tools of numbing entertainment and distraction, but so many don't have a purpose, meaning, and passion.*

Educators can't compete for students' attention when it comes to entertainment. Students have the tools of numbing entertainment and distraction, but so many don't have a purpose, meaning, and passion. Those missing pieces are exactly what teachers should offer, and are far more important, life-changing, and engaging than entertainment. Fighting entertainment for students' attention can feel like a losing battle, but there is hope!

» *Purpose* is when students clearly know what the learning goal is. They understand it is their job as learners to get there. Teachers help learners have purpose when they help them see the intended learning goals, like I discuss in chapter 1 (page 19).

» *Meaning* is developed when students feel like the work they are producing *matters*. The work feels authentic and useful. It's not about compliance or completion, but instead often about contribution toward the community or students' own future goals. Meaning comes when the learning really matters, and students see how their daily life and purpose aligns with their overall vision for the future. (I'll talk about how to help students create a vision in chapter 6, page 89.)

» *Passion* occurs when students care deeply about what they are learning or creating. They become excited and enveloped in the subject or content.

Where all three—purpose, meaning, and passion—merge, magic happens! This is where learners get lost in their work and lose all sense of time. Learning and creating can grip students, just like video games can. These *magical moments* (when students work to improve their skills from a place of purpose, meaning, and passion) can be *because* of the content they are engaging with and how the teacher delivers that content. Think about

> *Where all three—purpose, meaning, and passion—merge, magic happens!*

content as a medium with which teachers can create authentic and relevant opportunities for students to practice and develop skills and dispositions that matter. Or you can think about content as a vehicle that takes students to skill development and personal transformation. Let's look at another story that will help illustrate this.

## A Story About Will

A twenty-eight-year veteran social studies teacher never sent students to the office. She was a master-level, exceptional teacher. On this day, she opened my office door without a knock and told Will, a high school senior accompanying her, to sit down. He obeyed. I was the assistant principal at the time. I was surprised because this teacher never had discipline problems, but I was also just as surprised by who she brought.

Will wasn't a student who got in trouble. I knew him well. He was a sleepy-eyed student who sat in the back of my English classes when he was a freshman and sophomore. He was smart. He had thoughtful comments, but I had to wake him up a lot—when he bothered to show up, that is. He did just enough to get by.

The teacher said, "Mr. Hansen, you need to talk to Will about what happened in class. You can send him back, but you need to talk to him first." I got out a quick, "OK" before she spun around and started power walking back to her classroom. Then I turned to Will, who was visibly upset. When he had cooled a bit, I asked, "Will, what's going on?"

He said quietly, "I got upset."

"Yeah?" I asked, "What happened?"

He looked up and replied reluctantly, "Uh . . . I punched a hole in the wall."

I paused to take that in. "OK . . . . Why did you punch a hole in the wall?"

He restated his earlier answer, "Because, I got upset."

Feeling like I needed better questions, I replied quickly, "No, I gathered that! But *why* did you get upset, Will?"

Sheepishly he began explaining, "Well, we were having this debate in social studies class about the topic for a paper we are writing. I just got really fired up about it, so I punched the wall."

I sat for a moment, literally scratching my head, trying to make sense of what was happening. Then, I asked another dumbfounded question, "Wait. You mean to tell me, *you* got so fired up about a *debate* in social studies class that you punched a hole in the wall?"

"Um, yeah," he mumbled.

I was perplexed. Of all the people who were going to get that upset over a topic in social studies, Will would not have been even close to my first guess. Finally I said, "OK, three things, Will." He looked up at me. "Number one, don't punch holes in the wall anymore. Number two, you're gonna stay after school and help the custodian fix the wall." He nodded. "And, number three," I paused as I softened my tone to almost a whisper, "I want to see your paper when you get done writing it!"

Will got an *A* on his paper. Why? Because he suddenly cared about his grades? No, he didn't care any more about his grades while doing that assignment than he had for the previous twelve years. *He cared about what he had to say!*

## Worthy Content Supports Skills

Will's teacher was a master who understood what Will and his classmates needed most wasn't to have her deliver facts they could just as easily look up on their devices. Will's teacher understood what her students needed most from her academically was to help them develop essential skills that transcend any single unit or even any individual content area. These skills include, but are not limited to, the following.

» Sifting through vast amounts of informational text in various forms

» Determining what's credible and what's not

» Synthesizing texts

» Saying something new or old in a new or creative way

» Proposing a solution to a complex problem

» Citing evidence to support a claim

» Communicating those ideas in a medium that will reach an intended audience

» Having empathy for the audience, so students can speak influentially to their hearts and minds (Conley, 2010; Schlain & Let It Ripple Studio, 2015)

These are just some of the skills that transcend content and are absolutely necessary for students to learn to contend in the world.

Master teachers understand that despite some of the institutional pressure inherent with standardized testing accountability, content and discrete content-specific skills are no longer king. The goal must be skills that carry relevance across multiple disciplines. In an innovative economy, knowledge is no longer a scarce commodity—skills are (Wagner & Dintersmith, 2015). The next section also dives into the power of worthy content.

## Questions, Tasks, and Problems Worth Talking About

I often have the opportunity to observe classrooms in my work. One day, I walked into a sixth-grade classroom right after lunch. The teacher pulled out a book and started reading aloud. Without direction, students settled in right away to listen. I recognized the text. It was right toward the end of the book *Where the Red Fern Grows*. I was confused because that's not a sixth-grade-level book. However, like many others, I love that book! So, I sat in a comfy chair in the back of the room and just listened. After a few minutes, the teacher finished the book. Students discreetly wiped away a couple of tears, as did the teacher.

The teacher quietly gave the first piece of direction the students had received since they came in from lunch. "OK students, it's time for you to get into your writing groups and work on your essays." Gentle chaos ensued, but not the negative kind. It was the happy kind of chaos that takes place in a classroom where students are truly engaged in something they care about. Some students were standing, some unconsciously half-dancing about with energy. Some students were kneeling on their chairs with their elbows on their desks, leaning forward to talk to their peers. Some were talking too loudly. Some had their heads down, covering one ear with an elbow as they wrote.

While I was thrilled with the scene of engagement, I was still a bit bewildered. I wondered why this sixth-grade teacher was reading a fourth-grade book. I stood up to look around. Students came up to me, a stranger, and asked, "Hey, do you want to read my essay?" Yes, I did! I *really* did. I read a few essay drafts of considerable length. I was impressed. They were thoughtful, deep responses, citing valid evidence from the text, which I later found out was the essential skill this teacher's collaborative team was working on. The teacher's prompts for the different groups intrigued me even more. Some of her prompts were things like, "What is unconditional love?" "What is the relationship between sacrifice and love?" "What is *loyalty?*" "Does loyalty come at a price?" and "Why did the book have to end the way that it did to become a classic?" Sure, it was a fourth-grade text, but these rigorous questions were worthy of discussion.

The students wanted to talk about these questions, and they wanted to write about what they thought because they cared. The reason is because questions like these matter, especially to sixth graders. As students start to become self-aware, they want to understand life, what things are important, and where they stand in the middle of all of it. These prompts weren't just busywork or compliance-driven assignments; these prompts asked learners important questions, not about a book about a boy and some dogs, but about *themselves* and *life*! These questions are worth attention and effort to students, because in that classroom, they could feel the questions had weight.

Students were figuring out life—right there in a classroom—and they knew it. Their thoughts mattered. When I asked, these students could tell me the skill they were working on: "Citing evidence to back up a claim." They could explain why the skill matters, at least in the context of the current lesson. My teacher-heart warmed, and I joyfully walked out of that classroom. These were engaged students, owning their work, and their learning, just like Will. They had passion, purpose, and meaning in their work, and it all started with the content, the way the teacher presented that content, and the questions she asked.

My joy didn't last long. I walked to the very next classroom. There, the teacher was asking students to read and respond to released items from their state assessment as practice for "the test." Students were reading isolated and disconnected passages, and were then supposed to make a claim, using supporting evidence from the text. The teacher was chasing behaviors and exasperatedly trying to get students to write one or maybe two sentences. She looked frazzled and worn out as she repeated, "Come on guys, you need this. This is going to be on the test!"

Which class would you want your child in?

Content is the vehicle by which teachers can help students learn skills that matter, not just pass the test. Effective, wizard-like teachers use content to engage students deeply in extended discourse and debate. The purpose isn't necessarily deep learning of the content (although that does happen), but the development of essential skills.

Going back to Will's story, his teacher understood all this, so she used content to engage her learners deeply in extended discourse and debate. The purpose wasn't deep learning of the content (although that did happen), but the development of her students' skills as persuasive writers and speakers. Her passionate and masterful delivery of her content allowed her to engage students deeply. She used their engagement with and passion for the content as a means for cultivating ownership from students in developing their skills. Skills that, by the way, students need to contend in the world (Conley, 2010).

## Meaning Is a Powerful Motivator

*Meaning is perhaps the most powerful motivator.*

When students actually care about the content, their skill development takes on greater purpose for them. When they care about the content, their work has meaning. Meaning is perhaps the most powerful motivator.

Psychiatrist Viktor E. Frankl (2006), founder of *logotherapy* (a school of psychotherapy that describes a search for life's meaning), so beautifully explains this foundational human principle in his horrific story about surviving the WWII Nazi concentration camps. In his famous book *Man's Search for Meaning*, Frankl (2006) writes that if people have a purpose and meaning, they can endure endless challenges and immense suffering. In fact, Frankl (2006) believes people can even find joy amid the most terrible and trying of circumstances, if they have meaning. Most students don't endure such trying circumstances, but they still have the fundamental need for meaning—not just for surviving, but for thriving.

Somewhat contrary to Frankl's (2006) experience, Maslow (1943) proposes that people tend to satisfy their basic physiological needs (food and shelter) and safety needs before they can focus on other needs. Nonetheless, once those needs are met, people try to fulfill their needs for belonging and love. And the more those needs are met, the more intensely people feel the need to move toward the top of this hierarchy, which includes alignment with purpose and meaning, and fulfillment of potential in what Maslow (1943) called *self-actualization*. Purpose, meaning, and even passion are human needs! And, as one student clearly and succinctly stated after a discussion about purpose and meaning contrasted with forced compliance, "Compliance sucks!"

## Purpose-Driven Learning

I've had people come up to me after I've delivered a talk on purpose-driven learning and say, "Oh, what you're talking about is project-based learning." No, I'm talking about what I would call *purpose-driven learning*. I have seen too many instances where students and even teachers get lost in the weeds of a project. They lose sight entirely of the overarching learning goal of developing a specific essential skill. Wizards don't get lost. They create experiences and sometimes projects to engage students, but wizards always do it with their purpose at the center.

Not every lesson is going to be deeply engaging and inspire passion for content and skill development. And don't get me wrong, it is also necessary to teach a wide array of content, even if the rote learning of it isn't the ultimate goal. And it is wise to introduce and ensure students are comfortable with the format of most standardized tests. Just don't rely on tasks like those as your means for developing deep and lasting skills. If you do, you will end up forcing compliance, and holding points, grades, or privileges over students' heads. Students will likely feel bored, disengaged, and even victimized. Even *if* you get them to comply, students will forget what they've learned as quickly as they can and move on to the next task of momentary hoop-jumping compliance, just like they move on to the next new sixty-second experience on their smartphone (MIT Teaching + Learning Lab, n.d.).

Include some compelling questions or tasks to your selection of worthwhile content. The questions or tasks should be worth talking and writing about, solving, and creating representations about. The questions must give learners space for discourse. That means teachers can't be in search of just one answer. If there is a "right" answer, there is a "wrong" answer. This doesn't leave much room for taking risks. Students must feel safe exploring their thoughts, arguments, and solutions to complex problems, and have the opportunity to revise. Inherent in this type of discussion is *choice*. Students must have choice, though it should be within a framework. I'll go into depth about choice in chapter 4 (page 63).

You might wonder, does this apply to elementary learners as well? Yes, it does. Granted, it's usually easier to initially engage students in lower grades. If the teacher is just a little enthusiastic, students generally follow suit. But, without real engagement, these students lose interest quickly too. After reading a children's book, I have seen extraordinary conversations and discussions among kindergartners and first graders as they wrestle with big questions like, "Who makes a better friend, a spider or a turtle?" I have seen students get excited as they work on solving problems and explaining their solutions. I've seen versions of Socratic seminars. I've seen students pick up books way above their Lexile levels and wade through them because the students became passionate about the story or content.

## Selecting Content for Skill Development

Master teachers have a knack for choosing and using content that truly engages their students. They seem to intuitively know what they can use to capture students' attention. They also have a contagious energy, because when truly passionate people are talking about their passions, their enthusiasm is infectious. Students come alive in such classrooms. Not every text is world-changing and not every mathematics or science problem changes lives, and students will still engage with topics absent of deep life-meaning. However, the more teachers help students develop their skills outside the "drill and kill" model, and in more authentic and engaging ways, the more rapid and permanent the academic learning will be (MIT Teaching + Learning Lab, n.d.). The more learners engage in authentic learning experiences, the greater their opportunity to build skills such as self-efficacy.

Figure 3.1 provides some guidelines for selecting worthy content.

| Guidelines for Selecting Worthy Content |
|---|
| • Before you think about content, consider whether you are crystal clear about the intended learning goal for the period of learning, whether it's a day or a month. |
| • Determine what text, tasks, or activities would lend themselves to learning the overarching essential skill. In other words, what would really engage your learners and spark their passion? What do they care about? What is relevant in their world or community? |
| • Design questions and tasks with appropriate cognitive complexity that require critical thinking, problem solving, and creativity, and that do not have a single "right" answer. |
| • Select texts, videos, or other information that helps learners consider multiple perspectives and promotes empathy. Empathy helps learners consider the nuanced details of an issue. |
| • When possible, choose content that evokes an appropriate level of emotion. If content emotionally impacts people, they care about it, and will engage on a deeper level. |
| • Consider some of the important content within your curriculum, especially the content you know from past experience learners find engaging. Sometimes school or district leaders require teachers use certain scripted and highly-scheduled program materials. Even within that mandate, you can still choose the most relevant content and supplement as needed. |
| • Create opportunities to have learners present their work or solutions to an authentic audience when possible. |
| • Seek content or tasks that provide opportunities for the learning to be interdisciplinary, replicating the complexity of real-world problem solving. |
| • Allow learners to make choices about their learning, projects, or even content, or how they demonstrate proficiency on the intended learning goal. |

**FIGURE 3.1:** Guidelines for selecting worthy content.

*Visit **go.SolutionTree.com/instruction** for a free reproducible version of this figure.*

The following story illustrates the power of selecting worthy content. One of my favorite school projects when I was principal was the *Create Your Own Restaurant* project. There were some mathematics skills involved (like estimation, ratios, and budgeting), but it was an English language arts–centric project. The essential skills centered on persuasion, including tools of rhetoric, audience empathy, and presentation. Teacher teams clarified these learning goals for the students. Groups of learners could choose what kind of restaurant they wanted to create and, as a culminating project, they presented their restaurant idea to a panel of judges. The students' job was to convince the judges to "invest" in building their restaurant.

As the unit was about to begin that year, I had a young man I'll call Corbin, along with four friends, came to ask me a question. Corbin was in eighth grade and anything but shy. To be honest, he and his crew were in trouble *a lot*. Often the trouble was related to a lack of respect, backtalk, or defiance. Corbin and his friends could regularly be found late at night skateboarding on the steps of the school or across the street at the downtown park. "Hey Mr. Hansen, can we talk with you?" he asked with an unusually timid demeanor.

"Of course," I replied.

He stammered a bit at first and then his question came tumbling out, "You know how we have to create a restaurant?" I nodded. "Well see, the thing is we don't want to create a restaurant, but we really do want to open a skate shop someday. We talk about it all the time! Do you think we could create a skate shop instead of a restaurant?"

I looked at these boys, who had more than their fair share of troubles in life, including academic failures. They were hesitant, but hopeful as they asked me about something they cared about. I responded quickly, "Well, the unit is about persuasion. Talk to your teacher and persuade her!"

A couple of weeks later, I intended to find out when Corbin and his friends' presentation was scheduled so that I could go, but I didn't have to. Corbin came to see me the morning of. I almost didn't recognize him. His hair was neatly combed. He was wearing black pants that fit, unlike his usual too-big baggy pants. He had on a large white button-up shirt he borrowed from his older brother. We visited for a moment. He was pleasantly surprised that I wanted to come to his groups' presentation. Then he got a bit shy again. Hesitating, he said, "Mr. Hansen, the reason I came to see you this morning is 'cause I was just wondering . . . if it's OK, could I borrow a tie? I want to look my best."

I immediately started sliding the tie on my neck over my head as I said, "Absolutely, Corbin! You are more than welcome to borrow my tie!" He smiled.

Corbin and his friends presented their skate shop concept with passion, demonstrating their new persuasion skills. The detailed artwork they had created was inspiring, showing how much they cared and demonstrating an uncelebrated talent. They spoke, answered questions, and thoroughly impressed their panel, which readily agreed to "fund" their shop!

Here are a few key points that allowed Corbin and his friends to take ownership of their learning.

- » The teacher team communicated the learning goal of persuasion with clarity, including using video models.

- » Learners could make choices about the content, their presentations, and how they demonstrated their skills of persuasion.

- » The culminating task mattered to students because it was a real-life scenario, and because of that learning, the skill of persuasion mattered.

» The goals and tasks were relevant to learners and their community.

» The culminating task was cognitively complex, requiring critical thinking, problem solving, and creativity.

» There was purpose in their practice because they were working toward a final project.

» It was an interdisciplinary team effort.

» To be persuasive, they had to understand or have empathy for their audience.

» They had a real audience.

These factors allowed the students to take ownership of the project, and thus, take ownership of their learning.

## Concluding Thoughts

Schools no longer have a monopoly on education. Learners can learn almost anything, anywhere, at any time. Educators also can't compete on an entertainment level with all that's available to students. Students are used to making choices about vast amounts of content and their experiential lives, and they battle distractedness because of all that's available at their fingertips. So many of them are stuck in a compliance mindset and a story where school is oppressive, irrelevant, and obsolete. To counter that compliance mindset and the apathy that comes with it, teachers can provide purpose, meaning, and hopefully passion by engaging students in content that matters and is worthy of a hero's effort. That's when students wake up out of their haze, face the darkness of their potential to write the best essay of their lives, or deliver a truly persuasive presentation (and actually remember how to do it), thus transforming their skills and themselves into something more. That's the moment when students' work becomes authentic and has real meaning; they begin taking the stance of a hero.

# CHAPTER 4

# Facilitate Student Self-Assessment and Self-Correction

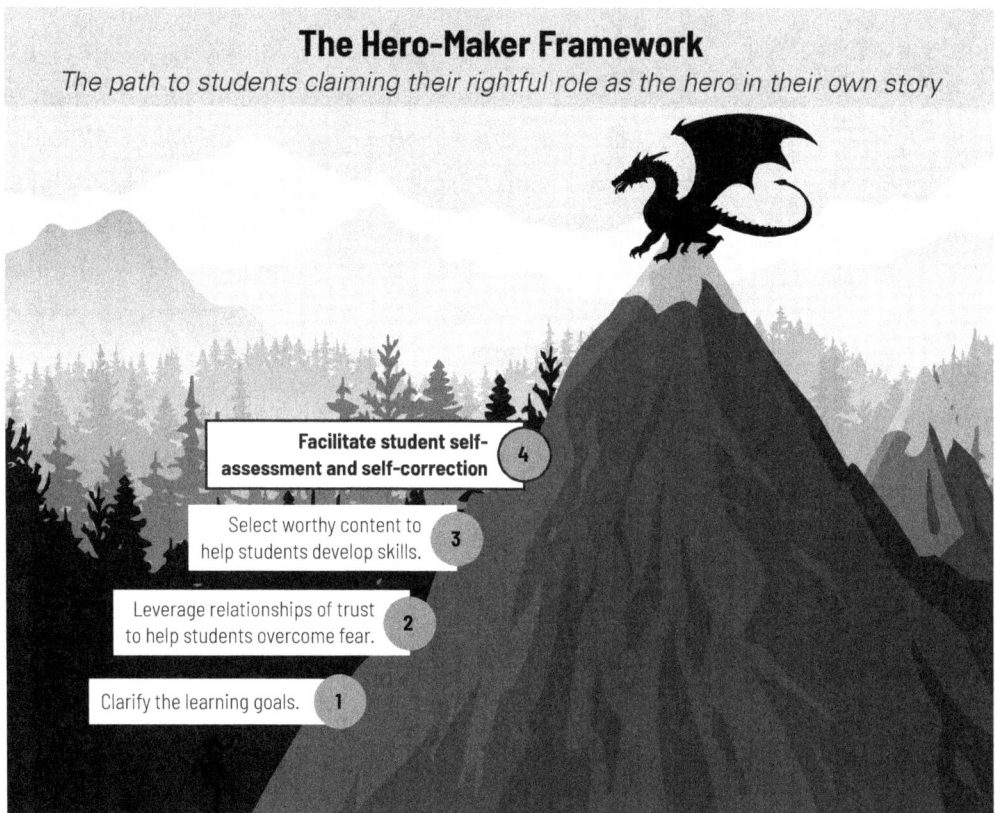

**The Hero-Maker Framework**
*The path to students claiming their rightful role as the hero in their own story*

**Facilitate student self-assessment and self-correction** 4

Select worthy content to help students develop skills. 3

Leverage relationships of trust to help students overcome fear. 2

Clarify the learning goals. 1

An essential step in the Hero-Maker Framework is moving away from the traditional feedback most educators are used to giving. Most teachers give *directive* feedback to learners. Instead, they should move toward giving learners *facilitated* feedback, or feedback learners provide themselves, often through teacher facilitation.

Though this may seem like a subtle change, it's hugely impactful (Brooks, Carroll, Gillies, & Hattie, 2019)! Teachers and learners should both be using data to track students' learning progress. Even in schools with strong collaborative teams (whose members embed assessment and feedback practices in their regular processes), tracking data is often a missing piece. Teachers in functioning collaborative teams conduct common assessments, analyze the results, and make intervention decisions based on data. But teachers often fail to provide learners with authentic or meaningful feedback (more than just a score). Teachers, not learners, examine the data and decide which interventions are appropriate. So, students may be getting help on the academic skills they need, but they are not empowered to direct their own learning. Students might get better, but from this stance, students are a product adults improve, not individuals empowered to improve themselves.

> *There are no mistakes or failures, only experiences we choose to learn from, or repeat until we learn from.*

This chapter walks you through the process of helping students self-select interventions based on their own assessment and make a plan for improvement. This is the mark of true heroes: students learn from their experiences, course correct, and keep trying until they reach their goal. There are no mistakes or failures, only experiences we choose to learn from, or repeat until we learn from. What teachers think of as failures are simply steps on the path to ultimate success.

In chapter 1 (page 19), I discuss how maps are useless if you don't know where you're going. However, a map is equally useless if you don't know where you are. Imagine standing on a dusty road with a paper map spread across the hood of your car. In this case, you're clear about where you want to go. However, if you don't know where you are, the map doesn't help you. This chapter is all about helping students see where they are in relation to a defined learning goal and helping them self-select their course for improvement to truly own their learning journey. If you know where you're going on the map and you know where you are, you can choose the course you will take.

First, let's challenge some traditional ideas about feedback.

## How I Used to Give Feedback

When I was a brand-new English teacher, I'm embarrassed to admit I didn't see a set of state standards for two years. I knew they existed, but I didn't go looking for them and no one handed them to me. That said, I wanted my students to be better writers.

I understood how important it is to be able to formulate ideas and communicate those ideas compellingly. I'm not sure I was any good at teaching writing, but my students worked on it a lot!

I knew the power of formative feedback, so I spent a lot of my time wandering around the classroom, looking over students' shoulders as they worked on their writing projects. I was enthusiastic. I would point and say something like, "I love what you're doing here! You might consider *XYZ* here." Students would look up at me and nod out of conditioned compliance. I quickly became frustrated because the students' writing wasn't really getting better. They weren't taking my feedback seriously. Even though I spent time giving feedback, it usually took me a while to get back to the same students (about three or four days later; I had a lot of students). I would look over the students' shoulders again when I made it back around and say, "Hey, I vaguely remember reading this essay, but what was the feedback I gave you last time?" They would look up at me blankly, shrug their shoulders, raise their eyebrows, and respond with something like, "Uh, I dunno." I was frustrated. My students were not owning the feedback and definitely were not owning their learning!

Then one day, in my frustration, something occurred to me. I was judging students for not owning the feedback and learning, but I could have easily leveled the same judgment at myself. I wasn't owning the feedback or learning either. The moment I gave students my feedback, it floated off into the ether. To be fair, I saw many students in a day! How could I be expected to remember the feedback I gave about each of their essays? I couldn't even remember where I parked most days, so remembering each student's essay wasn't going to happen.

So, accepting my limitations, I got a little smarter. I went to the dollar store and bought a clipboard. I put blank paper on my clipboard and started carrying it with me as I gave feedback. I practically chained that thing to my hand. Now as I wandered and gave feedback, I took quick shorthand notes about what each student might be struggling with. My notes were simple things like, *transitions need work*, *citations incorrect*, *thesis underdeveloped*, or *grammar poor*. I quickly started to notice patterns and the data I was collecting informed my practice. I learned what to reteach the whole class and also started pulling small groups to the back of the room based on common deficits. For example, I would call out the names of all students who needed to work on their transitions. Because I was pulling small groups, I was more efficient in my targeted intervention. Instead of giving sixty to ninety seconds to students as I looked over their shoulder, I could pull all the students struggling with transitions and spend seven, eight, or even ten minutes working with them. This was huge!

Things got better. My students' writing did improve . . . some, but there was still a problem. I was owning the learning (I was tracking the information and acting on it), but *learners* still didn't own the learning because they weren't tracking their data. In fact, as I called their names to come back to their small group, the students would march back with sighs, heavy footsteps, and slumped shoulders. To them, small-group work was a hassle. They resisted, like most do, when forced into compliance when they were without choice. They were getting better, but not on purpose. I was doing it *to* them. It was more efficient, but I was still directing the feedback.

## Shifting to Facilitated Feedback

How then, do I recommend offering feedback? Shift from *directed* feedback to *facilitated* feedback. In other words, instead of just *telling* students (directed) where they can improve and what to do to improve, help them *self-discover* (facilitated) where they are in relation to the learning goal, and give them options for how to improve. You can still wander around the classroom with a clipboard as students work on their writing (hopefully about excellent and authentic content, like I discuss in chapter 3, page 47), but your clipboard won't just hold blank paper.

### Progress Trackers

What should your clipboard contain? Figure 4.1 shows an example of a *progress tracker*. A teacher's progress tracker helps the teacher track progress of each learner while giving feedback and without necessarily creating an assessment event, like a quiz. But the tracker does much more than simply track scores or performance. Through a process I describe in chapter 7 (page 105), you will identify the typical pitfalls that trip up many learners on the path toward proficiency (or the steps they must master to be proficient). Educators generally call these pitfalls or steps *learning targets*. The tracker will help you quickly assess what help or intervention the learner needs in real time on which targets. This allows you to accurately guide learners as they make self-selected intervention decisions toward proficiency on the overarching skill or learning goal.

Notice how the overarching skill is being able to *Write arguments to support claims with clear reasons and relevant evidence*. This isn't easy; this skill is rigorous, complex, and has multiple targets or pitfalls embedded in it.

| Language Arts Progress Tracker (Teacher) | | | | | | | | | | | | | | | | |
|---|---|---|---|---|---|---|---|---|---|---|---|---|---|---|---|---|
| **Skill:** Write arguments to support claims with clear reasons and relevant evidence. | | | | | | | | | | | | | | | | |
| **Student Names** | **Learning Target 1.a:** Student can make and introduce a logical claim. | | | | **Target 1.b:** Student can support claim with clear reasons and relevant, credible evidence. | | | | **Target 1.c:** Student establishes and maintains formal style. | | | | **Target 1.d:** Student provides a concluding statement. | | | |
| Sarah | 2 | 2 | 3 | 3 | 1 | 1 | 2 | 2 | 2 | 3 | 3 | 4 | | | | |
| Juan | 1 | 2 | 3 | 3 | 1 | 1 | 2 | 2 | 2 | 2 | 3 | 3 | | | | |
| *4—above proficient or mastery level, 3—proficient, 2—not quite proficient, 1—far below proficient* | | | | | | | | | | | | | | | | |

*Source: Adapted from Hansen, 2015a; White Pine Middle School.*

**FIGURE 4.1:** Example of a teacher's progress tracker.

Use the progress tracker to collect on-the-fly assessment data specific to deficits you identified as pitfalls some students will likely need additional time and support to overcome. Write a score in each of the areas or targets as you make informal feedback rounds. Over time, you'll see what patterns emerge and also have a real-time record of progress for each individual learner. Good teachers have always given feedback, but great, intentional, empowering *wizard* teachers collect data *as* they give feedback. Wizards do this because they want to know in real time where each of their learners is and why. They are asking, "What part of the overarching skill is the student still struggling with?" and "What's holding the student back?"

The tracker helps teachers be systematic about assessing some of the typical pitfalls that a student has fallen into, which may be keeping the student from being proficient. It's not enough to know a student isn't proficient in the overarching skill. The real question is *why*. What's holding the student back? Which target or pitfall is the student falling into on the journey? Educators must know if they are going to provide *targeted* intervention specific to the student's deficit.

Following are some examples of how a teacher can facilitate feedback in the classroom, assuming the teacher has clearly established the overarching learning goal (as I discuss in chapter 1, p. 19), including using models of proficiency to clarify the learning goal through communication. Those models should be readily available if the teacher is going to engage learners in facilitated feedback. Don't skip this!

First, the teacher wanders around, progress tracker in hand, providing feedback to students.

> **Teacher:** "Hey, I love what you're doing here. When you look at the model of proficient work we went over in class, how do you think your work differs, or what do you need to improve?"
>
> **Student:** "I dunno."
>
> **Teacher:** "Well, get your model out. Let's look. What do you think of your claim?"
>
> **Student:** "I think it's a pretty good claim."
>
> **Teacher:** "I agree. It is a good claim. What about your evidence?"
>
> **Student:** "It seems good."

A typical response at first is likely to be something like "It's good," even if the evidence is clearly not "good." This is the moment of changing practice for most teachers. Resist the temptation of *directing* the feedback by *telling* the learner the evidence isn't "good," why, and what the learner should do to fix it. Instead, *facilitate* the feedback so the student self-discovers the need for improvement, as in the following example. The path for improvement is self-selected.

> **Teacher:** "Are you sure your evidence is solid? Look at your model. See the evidence? Remember those parts we color-coded that support the claim when we talked about what proficiency looks like as a whole class?"
>
> **Student:** "Yeah, I see it."
>
> **Teacher:** "OK, now look at your evidence."
>
> **Student:** "Oh, I see. My evidence isn't there yet."
>
> **Teacher:** "I agree, it's not there yet. I'm going to record your progress on my progress tracker on my clipboard, OK? Now, get out your progress tracker and make a note of where you're at."

A student tracker might also look something like figure 4.2. This example uses the following scale: 4—above proficient or mastery level, 3—proficient, 2—not quite proficient, 1—far below proficient.

| Name: *Juan Hernandez* | | 1 | 2 | 3 | 4 | 5 |
|---|---|---|---|---|---|---|
| **Essential Standard** | **Write arguments to support claims with clear reasons and relevant evidence.** | Date/ Score | Date/ Score | Date/ Score | Date/ Score | Date/ Score |
| **Learning Targets** | *This is my progress so far.* | *Sept 10* | *Sept 15* | *Sept 22* | *Sept 26* | |
| **1.a** | *I can make and introduce a logical claim.* | 2 | 3 | 3 | 3 | |

| 1.b | *I can support claim with clear reasons and relevant, credible evidence.* | 1 | 2 | 2 | 2 | |
|-----|---|---|---|---|---|---|
| 1.c | *I can establish and maintain formal style (including proper citations).* | 2 | 2 | 3 | 3 | |
| 1.d | *I can provide a concluding statement.* | 2 | 2 | 3 | 3 | |
| **Date** | **Looking at my data, what's my plan?** | | | | | |
| *Sept 26* | *I'm still struggling with credible evidence. I'm going to the What I Need (WIN) Time workshop about evidence with Mrs. Perez.* | | | | | |

Source: Adapted from Hansen, 2015a; White Pine Middle School.

**FIGURE 4.2:** Example of student's progress tracker.

Now, you *and* the learner are recording data about where the learner is on the learning journey. This is vital to empowering students to own their learning and move out of a compliance-driven or fixed mindset. Whoever owns the data owns the learning (Hansen, 2015). This is true of any worthwhile endeavor, particularly when the endeavor is difficult. If you have a serious goal, you track your progress toward that goal. Serious weight lifters not only carry a water bottle in the gym but also a notebook to record their progress. Serious athletes keep statistics to know where they need to improve. Serious teachers and serious learners track their data too.

## The Moment Students Are Truly Empowered

You've now helped the student notice the evidence the student provided "isn't there yet." This is the moment when students truly become *learners,* empowered with the responsibility and ownership of their journey. It's one moment when the hero answers the call.

**Teacher:** "OK, so your evidence is not quite proficient. (Pause.) What are you going to do about that?" (Pause.)

**Student:** "I dunno!"

**Teacher:** "This is your learning journey. You're not there yet. What are you going to do about that?"

**Student:** "I don't know! You're the teacher, aren't you supposed to teach me?"

**Teacher:** "No, you mistake my role here. This is your journey, not mine. I won't steal it from you! You're the learner here, not me. I already know how to do this. I've already walked this path and figured it out. It's your turn to do the same. It's your job to learn it! So what are you going to do about it?"

In that moment where you've challenged the student to answer the call of owning the learning, the student will likely balk. It's scary to take responsibility! Know what you will say, so this moment becomes the beginning of a serious shift out of dependence, compliance, and fear to independence, ownership, and courage. Don't steal the student's struggle. Instead, illuminate the student's options by offering choices.

> **Teacher:** "Well, you have some options. You can look at the model again and see if you can figure it out. You can talk with your group or your peers. Or it just so happens I'm going to be running a small group in the back of the room during the last ten minutes of class on this very target. If you'd like, you're welcome to join me."

*Don't steal the student's struggle. Instead, illuminate the student's options by offering choices.*

Now who owns the learning? You both do! You co-own it because you're both tracking it, but you've empowered the student to take ownership by tracking progress and making informed choices about *how* the student will improve. Students each see where they are in relation to the overarching learning goal (just like a on a map) because you've facilitated the feedback.

I often tell students, "If it was easy the first time, that just means it wasn't hard." They usually scratch their heads a bit at first, but then we talk about setting hard goals worth striving for. If it was easy the first time, the student wasn't stretching. We also usually end up having a conversation to reframe what *smart* is too. I explain being smart isn't already knowing how to do a thing: that's just prior exposure, luck, or even privilege. Instead, *smart* is not knowing how to do something and persevering until you do. It's noble and admirable to be that kind of smart; it's *heroic*. The Hero-Maker Framework helps students be that kind of smart, no matter where they start.

At first, students may need the teacher's support to shift from the sit-and-get feedback they are accustomed to. It may take some time for students to understand their right to ownership of the learning process; they aren't used to it. They may not be accurate in their self-assessment at first either. Teachers must make an investment of time on the front end to retrain students. But over time, students will become proficient at self-assessing, as long as they have a model to compare their work against. At that point, teachers can lead a whole-class conversation to help students self-select and determine their areas of need.

Follow up by helping students assess whether they have improved. How teachers frame intervention is vital to helping students take ownership. If teachers decide the intervention for them (without student choice or involvement), it will feel like school is being done to them. It will feel like it's about compliance, point chasing, and hoop jumping.

It's ideal if the intervention is also very fluid. For example, if a student with teacher help has selected an intervention to attend for the week and becomes proficient halfway through the week, get the student out! Ideally, send the student out *the moment the student is truly proficient.* Teachers want to signal to students that intervention isn't about compliance, "Show up here because I told you to!" Instead, teachers should signal that intervention is about learning the essentials: "The moment you learn this, you're out of here. Oh, and by the way, if you can figure out a way to learn the essential in the next unit efficiently and effectively, you won't have to come here in the first place." It's not that intervention is a punishment, teachers just want students to start owning their job as learners who must do more than just show up and do what the teacher tells them. They are powerful and capable and, with the right dispositions, they can shape their futures.

# A New Mindset

Once teachers are aware, they can see the monumental difference between directed and facilitated feedback, even though to the untrained eye, the teacher actions look similar. But just because teachers see the difference doesn't make it easy to make the switch. Remember, educators have years, even decades, of being conditioned to practice directed feedback through their own student and teaching experiences. They might be really good at it too, which likely is a comfortable place. Here are a couple strategies I suggest for teachers that may help you make the shift.

## Break the Old Habits

At first glance, this strategy may seem silly. I borrowed and adapted the concept from author and speaker James Clear (2018) and his book *Atomic Habits.* He suggests if you want to develop the habit of running in the morning, set your running shoes next to your bed so you practically trip over them when you get out of bed (Clear, 2018). At first, measure success simply by lacing up. If you get the shoes on your feet, it's a win. Similarly, if you want to get good at facilitating feedback and collecting information about where your learners are, get yourself a clipboard. Decorate it with your favorite stickers, whatever it takes to make it your own.

Here's the part that may feel silly, but will cue the change in habit. Next, take all your whiteboard markers and put them in a drawer where they are not easily accessible. Then grab your favorite marker, a piece of string, and some tape. Tape the string to your marker and tie the other end of the string to your clipboard. This means every time you reach for your whiteboard marker, you also have to be holding your clipboard in the other hand. It sounds silly, but old habits die hard and without some kind of deliberate consistency, the busyness of the day will lead to reversion back to familiar patterns. You must break the pattern! Having that annoying string and clipboard in hand will just help you remember to notice and record where your learners are and, hopefully, notice why.

> *Old habits die hard and without some kind of deliberate consistency, the busyness of the day will lead to reversion back to familiar patterns.*

Voilà! You've laced up! You are now collecting actionable, real-time information you can use about where your students are and why they are there. You also now have actionable data to bring to your collaborative team meeting to advocate for specific intervention workshops without having an assessment. You're getting that information with extraordinarily little extra effort if you're already used to giving regular feedback, and especially if you're being intentional about moving to facilitating feedback instead of directing feedback.

## Visualize the Shift

The second strategy is less practical in nature, but particularly powerful when making the shift in how you think about effective feedback. Simply write a reflection as if you are in the future, after you have made the desired shift to facilitated feedback.

Following are a few prompts to help you write the reflection.

» Here's how I used to give feedback . . .

» What I now know about the power of facilitated feedback is . . .

» Here's how I now give feedback . . .

I highly encourage you to take the time to write this reflection. It's designed to give you a jump start on changing behavioral habits by changing your mind or the way you think.

Shifting from directed to facilitated feedback is probably one of the hardest changes teachers will make as they adopt the Hero-Maker Framework. When teachers see students making errors, it can be exceedingly difficult to resist jumping in to help instead of coaching students to see what the teachers already see. Helping is part of who teachers are. They must change their minds about what the best way is to really help students.

When people create new habits, they actually create new synaptic connections or neuropathways in the brain matter (Huberman, 2022). Your brain changes, but your brain doesn't conceptualize time the same way your mind has been conditioned to (through a social construct). So by thinking about the future, particularly writing about it as if you have already adopted the new habit, will help prime the change. You're not tricking your brain; you are helping your brain step away from old, conditioned beliefs about teaching and start to form new neuropathways to support the development of new habits that align with new beliefs about learning and your role in giving feedback.

## A Story About Kindergarten

Westland Elementary is a small elementary school doing big things. Named a national Model PLC school (visit www.allthingsplc.info), the teachers there have worked hard to transfer ownership of learning to students. Shalynn, a kindergarten teacher, relayed the following story about one of her students during one of my visits.

Sophie is as cute as they come, but at age five, she already has big challenges—so much so that Shalynn couldn't get Sophie out from under her desk for the first few weeks of school. Sophie wouldn't try to learn her numbers or letters, seemed fearful, and already exhibited strong fixed mindset tendencies. Shalynn stayed patient and kept working on building a relationship of trust. Eventually, Sophie came out from under the desk and started to learn her letters, one at a time. Shalynn, a serious learner herself, was helping all her students, including Sophie, track their own progress. Sophie started to experience some small gains and could see her progress. Shalynn engaged Sophie in a number of metacognitive conversations (see chapter 5, page 79), and Sophie grew more confident. Then, Sophie started doing her work at her desk instead of hiding under it.

I often share with audiences a recorded exchange between the two that Shalynn gave me for the purpose of helping others see the power of this work. Sophie's young voice comes through, clearly excited. She talks about her sight words. Her teacher, a true wizard, asks her how many she has learned (or where she is on the learning journey). Sophie talks about all the words she has learned, categorized into short lists, from her progress tracker.

Shalynn asks supportively and with enthusiasm, "How'd you do it? How'd you learn so many?" Then with sincere curiosity, making Sophie the hero who gets to tell her story about how she overcame challenges, Shalynn listens intently.

Sophie sounds like a ray of sunshine as she sings, "I practiced and now I know them!"

Her wizardly mentor approves and then asks her, "What's next, Sophie?" Sophie explains with new confidence, borne out of experience, that she is on list sixteen and will go all the way through twenty, counting each list as she points to her progress tracker. Figure 4.3 (page 74) shows an example of a student progress tracker a student like Sophie might create.

| List 1 | List 2 | List 3 | List 4 | List 5 |
|--------|--------|--------|--------|--------|
| ☑ the | ☑ for | ☑ at | ☑ to | ☐ do |
| ☑ in | ◯ I | ◯ go | ◯ not | ☐ did |
| ☑ my | ☑ am | ◯ it | ◯ can | ☐ too |
| ☑ a | ☑ here | ☑ like | ☐ you | ☐ will |
| ☑ is | ☑ and | ☑ be | ☐ are | ☐ with |
| **List 6** | **List 7** | **List 8** | **List 9** | **List 10** |
| ☐ all | ☐ say | ☐ down | ☐ our | ☐ we |
| ☐ me | ☐ now | ☐ they | ☐ who | ☐ he |
| ☐ was | ☐ have | ☐ that | ☐ where | ☐ she |
| ☐ no | ☐ said | ☐ this | ☐ what | ☐ but |
| ☐ so | ☐ come | ☐ ate | ☐ must | ☐ want |

**FIGURE 4.3:** A sample kindergarten student progress tracker.

Sophie knows it was hard, but she also knows she overcame the challenge. She has a confidence that didn't exist before her teacher empowered her. Sophie's confidence isn't reliant on her teacher though. She sees what is next: "Sixteen, then seventeen, then eighteen . . . ." She is not scared or overwhelmed looking at those challenges or seeing them as scary dragons. Instead, she is confident in facing them precisely because she has faced similar ones in the past. Her confidence is based on her newly formed experience and subsequent story about herself. Sophie *knows* she can. When you know the context for this young learner, listening to the exchange she has with her teacher is enough to bring tears to your eyes. As I share this and countless other stories like it, I've come to understand that the tears of audiences are joyful tears. They are tears of hope, both for Sophie and the new hopeful possibilities for teachers too. This kind of transformation is not only possible but also reliable and repeatable. It simply works! Progress just feels good, especially for students like Sophie, who have struggled in the past.

## The Physiological Reward for Progress

With every step of progress toward a goal, there is a physiological reward in the form of a release of dopamine. Popular media refers to *dopamine* as one of the "feel-good hormones" (Psychology Today, n.d.). More accurately, it's a *neuromodulator* that plays a key role in pleasure and reward. Neuroscientist Andrew Huberman (2021) explains just one of the roles of dopamine: "Dopamine release reinforces the neural circuits that led to that reward. So the next time we're in that situation, those circuits fire more strongly and we're likely to repeat the behavior that led to the reward." The drive for dopamine is behind almost all people's motivations, behaviors, and even addictions (Huberman, 2022).

There are healthy ways to chase the release of dopamine, and there are less-healthy ways. Unlike unhealthy supplies of dopamine, the steady supply of healthy dopamine lies in working for it through achievement, but in different ways than most people think.

There is a surge of dopamine when you achieve a long sought-after goal, such as graduation from a graduate program. It feels good, but oddly enough, the feeling doesn't last long. In fact, there is a dopamine drought shortly after reaching a serious goal that leaves the achiever with a bit of an empty feeling, asking, "Now what? What's next?" (Huberman, 2022). The steadier, more consistent, and sustainable supply of dopamine is in demonstrable *progress* toward achievement. In other words, the "feeling good" or joy really is in the journey, not the destination. It's trite, but it's true! Huberman (2022) explains:

> So even if you're not achieving the ultimate goal, if you're making progress, you're getting dopamine. And so what we want to do is create a dopamine escalator, where you're getting dopamine all the time as you're making progress toward your goal. And that's what keeps you motivated and engaged.

This has profound implications for the way savvy teachers think about students and how they attempt to motivate them. Those who figure out this connection rarely have student motivation problems anymore.

The takeaway here is even your most seemingly unmotivated students are hardwired with a physiological motivation reward as they make progress toward a defined goal! That's powerful. It's most powerful if the students can see their progress: where they started, where they are, and where they are going. One of the absolute best ways educators can help students do this is to help them track their own progress. Remember, *whoever owns the data, owns the learning.*

> *Even your most seemingly unmotivated students are hardwired with a physiological motivation reward as they make progress toward a defined goal!*

## Doing the Work

The dialogues in this chapter serve as models for your own conversations to help your learners self-assess and self-select the intervention they need. Following are the bones of this process.

1. Help students clearly see the overarching learning goal through the use of models of proficiency.

2. Help students see where their current performance is in relation to the defined learning goal, using facilitated feedback.

3. Help students track their progress.

4. Help students decide what they will do to improve in any specific areas of need.

Figure 4.4 is a self-assessing and self-selecting intervention template that will help you and your learners get used to the process. But beware: handing out the template and telling students to fill it out makes it nothing more than another compliance worksheet. Teachers must explain the purpose and model the process. Some students will be able to use the template effectively right away, while others will need extra attention and facilitation. The version in figure 4.4 includes notes and helpful dialogue starters.

---

**Student Self-Assessing and Self-Selecting Intervention Template**

**Directions:** Use the following questions to self-assess your progress and determine what you'll do next to improve your learning.

---

When I look at the model and my work, I think where my current performance is strong.

**Teacher dialogue starter:**

"OK, looking at your own work and the model, where do you think your current performance is strong?"

**Note:** It's OK to point out strengths in performance and provide compliments as long as you don't overpraise or are disingenuous.

---

Looking at the model and my work, I think where my current performance is falling short.

**Teacher dialogue starter:**

"OK, looking at your own work and the model, where do you think your current performance is falling short? How is your work different from the model?"

**Note:** At first, it's difficult for teachers to switch from directing feedback to facilitating self-discovered feedback. It's just as difficult for students to switch from being passively given feedback to taking an active role in self-assessing; they may need a little help at first. Stick with it. It takes practice.

---

Make sure to record your scores on your progress tracker!

**Teacher dialogue starter:**

"Now, get your progress tracker out. What do you think? What score are you going to write to record where you are in your progress? I'm writing the same thing on my progress tracker that I keep for you."

**Note:** It's vital for a later step in developing self-efficacy that students track their progress. Students should see where they started, where they are, and where they are going. Don't skip this step!

My plan for improving is _____

**Teacher dialogue starter:**

"OK, you've decided that you're not there yet with the XYZ target. Not yet! Is that right? (Pause for confirmation.) OK . . . (pause and give your full attention to the student). So, what are you going to do about that?"

**Note:** It's important not to let students off the hook with the typical, "I dunno." It's imperative that you keep putting the onus of responsibility and control back on them. Many will try to get you to pick up their responsibility. Resist! Say, "This is your learning journey! And this skill is essential to your future. You're not there yet, so what are you going to do about it?" Pause and listen. Give choices. "You have some options. Here are your choices _____. What do you think?"

**Note:** It's important for students to track their progress from beginning to end. Seeing demonstrable progress provides the dopaminergic motivation they need and is vital to metacognitive reflection later (see chapter 5, page 79)—a key to building true self-efficacy.

**FIGURE 4.4:** Self-assessing and self-selecting intervention template.

*Visit **go.SolutionTree.com/instruction** for a free reproducible version of this figure.*

The intention in this example is to move from *directed* to *facilitated* feedback. Coach students so they see their current position in relation to a defined learning goal. (Where is their arrow hitting in relation to the target? Or where are they on the map in relation to their clearly marked destination?) Help students self-assess to figure out what's holding them back. Once they see *which targets* are keeping them from being proficient, they can choose (with your help at first) which interventions are most beneficial to reaching the goal. It's important for students to choose! It's also important for you to provide options for them to choose from.

The best progress trackers allow students to record their skills over a period of time. The more frequently students track their progress, the better the opportunity for them to see the progression of their growth. It gives learners a chance to feel that little dopamine surge, so long as teachers have them in their ZPD and they are making steady progress.

For more discrete, but essential skills (such as letter recognition, mathematics fact memorization, or knowing high-frequency sight words), the teacher will likely not need to refer back to a model but instead use the progress tracker frequently.

## Concluding Thoughts

Making the shift to facilitated feedback from directed feedback isn't easy for students or teachers. For students, it's a shift from a passive to an active role in directing their learning. It's easier to passively wait for someone to tell you what to do than it is to perform the cognition necessary to evaluate your own performance and decide how to improve. They must own and lead their learning by making decisions and acting; there is more responsibility in ownership and leadership. It's uncomfortable to be responsible and lead when you're not used to it, so students may resist at first. Many have years of conditioning to reinforce their compliant passivity.

For teachers, as the primary distributors of learning, letting go of an inherited, conditioned role and the accompanying control is tough. It's quicker to just tell students what to do, but that doesn't empower them. Doing the work for them makes students dependent and doesn't honor them as the heroes they are. To really make the change stick, teachers should change their own mindset about the role of students. They are not passive students anymore; they are powerful learners and heroes who need a wise facilitating mentor to see them as such. The more teachers make the shift from *teaching* and *directing* to *facilitating learning* and *guiding learners*, the less concerned they become with teaching a great lesson, and more concerned with working with each learner to understand where the learner is and then help the learner own the choices for improvement.

To own your choices or be in charge of your learning journey, you must know where you're going. You also must know where you stand. When you do, you're empowered to make choices about *how* you go from where you are to where you want to be. Tracking the progress of the journey is important for motivation, but it serves an even more important purpose in the Hero-Maker Framework. It's through the experience of tracking progress that teachers help students literally tell a new story about themselves—one where they are the hero of their own learning journey. I'll explain how in chapter 5 (page 79).

# Use Metacognition to Change Mindsets

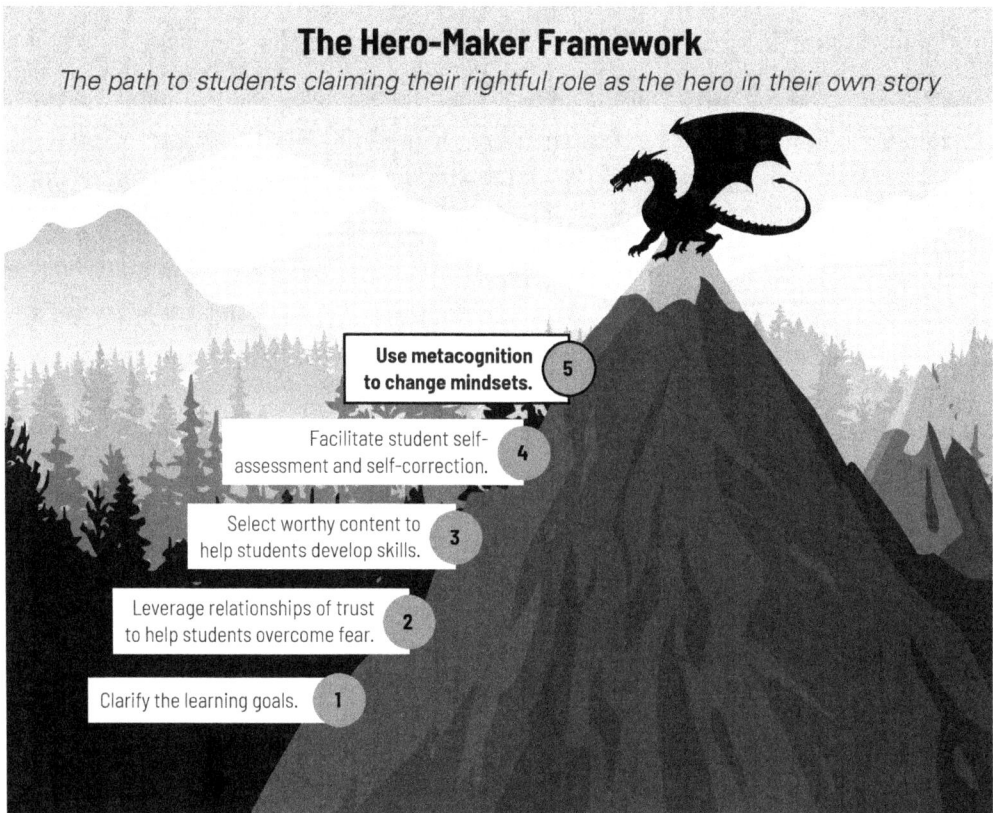

**The Hero-Maker Framework**
*The path to students claiming their rightful role as the hero in their own story*

5 — Use metacognition to change mindsets.

4 — Facilitate student self-assessment and self-correction.

3 — Select worthy content to help students develop skills.

2 — Leverage relationships of trust to help students overcome fear.

1 — Clarify the learning goals.

**M**etacognition is a game changer when it comes to helping learners believe in their own capabilities. This step helps learners trade in a fixed or compliance mindset for a hero mentality. It helps students see themselves differently. I'll begin by defining the term and then dive a little deeper.

The term *metacognition* is thrown around a lot in education. It's usually reduced to something like "thinking about your thinking" or "reflecting on your learning." It's sort of a buzzword. Educators know using metacognition is good, but are often unsure of its purpose and what it looks like. Metacognitive strategies help immensely with retention of academic learning (Hattie, 2023). But, as important as that might be, for the purposes of this book, engaging students in metacognition provides an even more profound reason than just retention.

Teachers want to help students metacognitively reflect on their learning progress and processes to inform themselves about *themselves*. Metacognition helps students reflect on their progress, processes, and efforts so they clearly see what they've achieved and experienced. Using their new experiences of success or progress (which teachers help facilitate), learners can tell a new story about themselves as a hero based on the evidence. Engaging students in metacognition will help them discover that new story.

Employing metacognitive conversations and other strategies helps students reflect on and understand the causal relationship between their effort and their progress. You might hear, "Because I tried and persevered, I made progress. Maybe I'm stronger than I think." However, it isn't just the experience of real progress that changes students' story about themselves. It is the *reflection* about the progress and how they did it that creates the space for students to write a new narrative in their minds about what they are capable of. The educator's job is to create that space for students.

> *Employing metacognitive conversations and other strategies helps students reflect on and understand the causal relationship between their effort and their progress.*

The following section relates the power of metacognition, which became evident during a conversation I had with a student while I was still serving as a principal.

## A Story About Donny

The bell rang and a swarm of students buzzed in the halls. I locked eyes with Donny, a seventh grader I knew well, amid the many others who were busily chatting and bustling toward their next class. Donny's floppy hair matched his disheveled clothes, which I noticed he had worn the day before. His untied shoelaces slapped back and forth as he galloped toward me and came to a sudden halt. "Mr. Hansen, Mr. Hansen! I passed my science quarterly assessment!" he blurted.

"You did? Nice! Way to go!" I gave him a high five. I could have overpraised him or told him to get an ice cream certificate at the office. Instead, I squared up to give my full attention to him and asked him to tell me his story, "Tell me about it, Donny!" I listened intently.

Thrilled to share his success, Donny whipped open a navy blue three-ring binder. I recognized it from the supply closet. Donny was a nice kid. He never got in trouble, but he wasn't a student who was typically academically successful, and his family wasn't going to be buying him a binder. He rifled through his papers to find his progress tracker. His teacher was only in her second year, but she was already a master at helping students track their progress. She was a coach, familiar with keeping statistics and helping her learners to do the same. Donny started from the top, about to tell me every detail of the unit. I redirected him: "Where was your struggle, Donny? What part was hard?"

He slid his finger down and pointed at one of the targets, "Well, we were learning about Punnett squares. When we started this unit, I was lost. I thought this was way too hard for me, and I would never get it!" Unsolicited, he pointed at his progress tracker. "See, this is where I started," as he pointed to the first score. "I bombed the preassessment!"

I listened intently as he went on telling his story. He pointed at multiple formative scores he had recorded for this particular target on his tracker: "1, 1, 1, 3 . . . "

I asked as he pointed at the first 3 in the progression, "What happened here?"

"I finally got it!" he blurted.

"No, I get that, but how did *you* do it, Donny? This was hard, right?" He furrowed his brow in concentration as he remembered. He said his teacher had pulled him to a small group in the back of the class.

"What else?" I asked. She had talked with him, one to one.

"What else?" He talked with his partner.

"What else?" With the teacher's help, Donny had self-selected to go to an intervention group specific to Punnett squares during *CAT time*, a schoolwide intervention block named after our mascot and targeted for Tier 2 support.

"I get that Donny, but you're telling me all about the activities you did. What was your part? How did you really *do* it?" I asked as I stared him in the eyes and listened fiercely.

He looked up at me incredulously, like he wanted to say, "How do you not get this?" He was almost yelling as he put his hand on his hip, "Well, Mr. Hansen, I *tried,* really hard!"

I nodded, and spoke slowly as I chose my words carefully, "Oh, I see! So . . . you mean to tell me that your *effort* had something to do with your success?"

His eyes looked up and to the left while he thoughtfully weighed my words and then responded with a firm nod, "Well, yeah, Mr. Hansen!"

I nodded back slowly, showing my own exaggerated thoughtfulness so he knew we were having a moment. "That's interesting! That's so interesting!" I said slowly, hoping it was sinking in that *he* was the key to his own success. "Donny, do you think this applies to any other areas of your life too? Like future challenges?"

He stood still for a moment considering, "Yeah . . . maybe."

I replied, nodding, "Yeah, Donny, maybe." Donny and his shoelaces flopped away toward his next class.

Donny, like me, will likely forget everything he learned about Punnett squares. But years later, he will continue to carry with him what experiences like this one taught him—that through his dogged effort, he is the master of his learning. He is the hero in his story. He can learn, unlearn, and relearn what he needs to be successful. I hope Donny can say and mean, "I can do hard things! The reason I know I can is because I've done them before." This is the gift, above all others I would give to Donny, my own children, and every other student: *self-efficacy*!

In Donny's case, the data were essential to the metacognitive conversation. His progress tracker was at the center of his story. The tracker painted a picture, providing tangible evidence, a record of his journey, and eventual triumph. Without progress monitoring, students won't be able to see how far they have come.

## How to Have a Metacognitive Conversation With Students

The following are some suggestions for engaging your students in metacognition related to their academic work.

### How Did You Do It?

Ask your students, "How did you do it?" or "Tell me about it!" Pay close attention to their answers and be as excited as you would be if they were telling you about an epic adventure while sitting around a campfire. Your attention gives their story credibility and importance. Make them the expert. Make them the hero. Then, listen like it's the most important thing you've ever heard them say, because it probably is.

Ask probing questions like, "Was it hard at first?" Help students identify the part of their story where they (the heroes) got knocked down in the dirt, but got back up again—that's the part you're trying to tease out. Ask, "Where did you struggle? How did you overcome it? What did you do?" Remember, heroes get up and try again when they've failed. That's it. Help students tell about the time when they persevered. Ask if they were scared or if it was hard: "Then what happened? How did you do it? How did you make progress?" Listen and help each student tell a proper story.

## I Knew You Could

Don't overpraise the accomplishment, as too much praise can feel insincere. Overpraise also communicates surprise in the accomplishment. You shouldn't be surprised when students do the thing you said you believed they could do. If you do overpraise, students will subconsciously pick up on what feels like a lack of integrity. Praise it once and sincerely, "Nice work!" and say with the confidence of a future-seeing wizard, "I knew you could do it."

While students are telling their story, it's hard not to talk too much, but you must resist. This is their story; you're just helping students tell it by asking the right questions. The most essential realization teachers hope students will make is that their effort leads to progress. When students notice it, your job is to just notice it too. Draw attention to the relationship between their effort and their success or progress. "So, you mean your effort had something to do with your progress?" This is when the most tender-hearted teachers are tempted to overpraise—*don't*. Just notice and help students notice that their effort is the key.

## What's Next?

Once students notice the connection between effort and success, pause. Let this knowledge sink in and then ask, "What's next?" Help students use the dopamine-induced high (borne out of progress) to orient toward their next immediate challenge. Life isn't about facing one big dragon, but a series of tests or facing thousands of little dragons. Learners don't have to face their fears all at once, just the next one. There will always be another dragon waiting ahead, but fear doesn't have to be the dominant emotion. Past experiences help learners have the courage to face new challenges, confident they will overcome them, precisely because they have in the past. Reflecting helps solidify the new story the students are telling themselves about themselves.

The moral to this story (and what educators want students to take away) is this: *If I give real effort, use good strategies, and stick with it long enough, I will make progress.* Think of this as an equation:

Effort + Good Strategies + Time = Progress (Success)

*Life isn't about facing one big dragon, but a series of tests or facing thousands of little dragons. Learners don't have to face their fears all at once, just the next one.*

Following is a list of prompts to help you engage students in a metacognitive conversation. The key isn't the questions, but to listen fiercely to their answers. Help students tell a story about how they overcame the hard parts—the parts where they kept trying despite being knocked down in the dirt. Don't overpraise or overtalk, just listen with your eyes, pay full attention, and notice the accomplishment.

» Tell me your story!

» How did you do it?

» What did you do?

» What was the most difficult part?

» Where did you feel like you got knocked down in the dirt?

» Were you scared?

» What did you tell yourself when your first attempts failed?

» How did you move forward?

» What advice would you give someone else struggling with the same things?

» What was the key to your progress?

» How hard did you try?

» Did your effort have something to do with your success?

» What strategies worked well?

» What strategies didn't work well?

» What do you notice about where you started?

» What were your emotions when you started?

» How do you feel now?

» What does this mean for future challenges?

» How does your experience inform your future learning process?

» What's next?

» What does this mean about you?

If possible (without becoming awkward), after students tell you their story, ask them to repeat the following phrase after you:

> I can do hard things. I know this because I've done them in the past.

## Metacognition in the Classroom

Teachers can lead metacognitive reflection one to one for an individual, or for a whole class or peer to peer—and even for student self-directed reflection. Students fill out reflection sheets to help them reflect on their learning process. This might be all that it takes for students who are predisposed to self-efficacy. However, you may find the need to differentiate your support for students whose experiences have been contrary to the development of a story rooted in self-efficacy.

Some students will need you to hear their reflection and story in an individual conversation more than others. The only way some students will know their story matters and is believable is because you give time to hearing it and paying attention to it. Students who have struggled with a negative story will need some guidance to break their old programming. These students may not believe the new evidence right away. As a witness, your attentive listening adds credibility to the new evidence.

There are some wizardly teachers and coaches who have extrapolated the idea of metacognition to bolster student efficacy *before* actual achievement. These learners already have some efficacy experiences in their past. Teachers have their students tell or write a story about themselves overcoming an upcoming academic or even physical challenge. They help their students experience future success by telling a story as if the achievement is in the past. The students anticipate possible challenges, obstacles, and even fears they will face and overcome. By having students envision their success *before it occurs*, teachers help students take a step toward their potential.

> *By having students envision their success before it occurs, teachers help students take a step toward their potential.*

## Climbing the Mountain

Imagine you're tasked with climbing an exceedingly high mountain. You don't believe you can, but you have a guide. Your guide believes in you, and you trust her competence and judgment. So, when your guide asks you to take just a few steps, you do. With her encouragement, you take a few more, and a few more, and then a few more. Hours later, during a water break, your guide engages you in a conversation. Although you are not at the top of the mountain, she asks you to turn and look at how far you've come. It's the first time you've looked back. You're amazed and a little proud at how high you've climbed! Sure, you had help (through your guide's encouragement and maybe a safety rope at times), but it was your effort that brought you to these dizzying heights. You did this! You feel the accomplishment when you look back. There may be more to climb ahead, but now you know you can, precisely because you already have.

Without progress data to reflect on, when you ask students to turn around and see how far they've come, it's like a thick wall of fog has rolled in. They don't see where they started nor how far they've come. And students won't remember a time when they didn't know how to do what they now know how to do. They might downplay how scary it was for them to face the challenge. They might try to discount the achievement by attributing it to luck or talent or even by giving credit to you or the task itself: "Yeah, but that wasn't that hard. That part was easy." In this instance, remind students: "Yeah, it's not that hard for current you, but for two-weeks-ago you, this was beyond tough! Don't you remember? What do your data say?" The tracking data enable the full power of the metacognitive conversation and realization—or when students make the connection that their progress is a result of their effort. Don't let students off the hook by allowing them to say, "It was easy."

I'm not inherently a numbers guy. I don't get warm and fuzzy feelings about numbers like some do, but I do get extremely passionate about students tracking their progress. I understand the potential power for transformation when students track their own progress and tell their story about it.

## Concluding Thoughts

Some months after Eddie went down the giant slide, we drove back through that same town and Eddie begged me to stop. There are many slides in the world, but that one had meaning for him. It was there that he faced a gripping fear. On the other side of that fear was something of great value, the transformational knowledge about himself: *he could face his fears.* When we found the old park, Eddie bolted for the top of the slide and promptly slid down. I smiled because this time, Eddie enjoyed a long slide in a sunny park, no dragons to fear in sight. Eddie had made "friends" with his dragon, and now he and his dragon were playing together.

While he sat perched to go down the slide again, I asked, "Eddie, do you remember when you learned how to go down the slide? How did you do it?" He told me his story of incremental progress up the slide while he pointed at each spot of his advancement. I listened intently. I asked if it was scary at first. He nodded, remembering the fear. I said, "Sometimes things are scary at first, but when you face those things, what happens?"

He gave me a thumbs-up, high above his head and smiled while he chirped, "Good stuff!"

"Yeah!" I agreed, "Good stuff." He pushed off, gliding joyfully down the gravity-fueled delight another time. Eddie stood when he reached the bottom and did a silly, happy dance, just like any six-year-old conquering hero should.

Eddie was starting to understand that with a little courage and a little perseverance, even if he struggled at first, he could do hard things. He was becoming the hero of his own story, just like everyone is constantly and forever becoming the hero of theirs. On rare occasions (like Eddie with the slide), I have seen this same excitement in students as they hurriedly pull their parents into their classroom, the place of their triumph, and, in turn, transformation occurred. Often their parents don't see why this classroom is so special; it looks like all the others. But students are so proud to show their parents their accomplishment and the classroom where the accomplishment happened. Such classrooms (and scary slides) are sacred, so show reverence when learners want to show them to you.

When learners develop true self-efficacy, they are confident in the knowledge they can do hard things precisely because they have done so in the past. It's not that students quit feeling fear when they face challenges. They just know they can face those fears. It's their conclusion based on their evidence of experiences. Self-efficacy is a developable disposition for this very reason. Above all others, your role as a teacher or wizard is to help students develop self-efficacy. Metacognition will be one of your most powerful tools. If the Hero-Maker Framework were a story, metacognition is the climax in the plot. It's the very spot where students learn to see themselves differently.

# CHAPTER 6

# Help Students Create a Compelling Vision

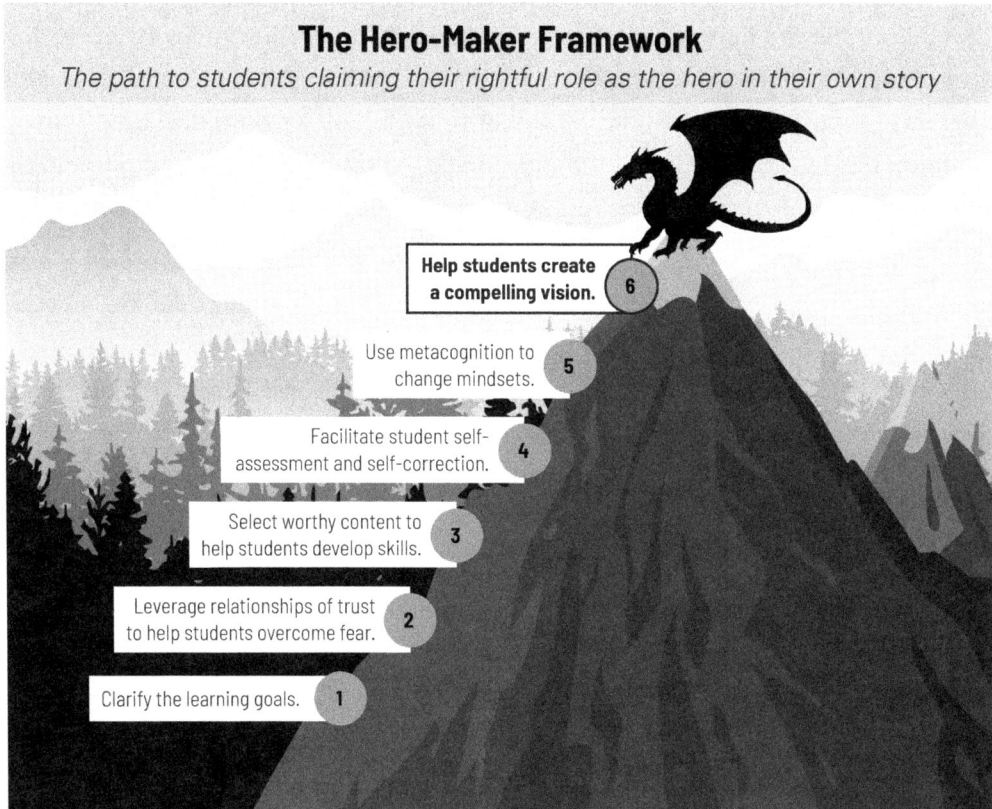

**The Hero-Maker Framework**

*The path to students claiming their rightful role as the hero in their own story*

Help students create a compelling vision. **6**

Use metacognition to change mindsets. **5**

Facilitate student self-assessment and self-correction. **4**

Select worthy content to help students develop skills. **3**

Leverage relationships of trust to help students overcome fear. **2**

Clarify the learning goals. **1**

The sixth and last step of the Hero-Maker Framework is to help learners begin to develop a vision for their future. This is not to be confused with step one, which I cover in chapter 1 (page 19): students need to see the learning goal they're aiming at. When students can see their learning goal, it provides them with clarity and an intentional purpose for reaching the goal. But it's a short-term goal, lasting only as long as the unit. True heroes who own their journey see beyond the short term. They must see how all their work to achieve their short-term learning goals (and the self-development that comes with achieving them) is in service of a larger vision for their future.

Bandura (1997) explains a *vision* serves as a guide that helps a learner choose how to develop specific capabilities. Tony Robbins (n.d.) explains *developing and focusing on a vision* "means determining the way you want your life to go. To create a life where you're thriving, not just surviving, you must focus on creating a compelling future." Born into slavery in the 1860s, George Washington Carver, a hero in his own story, overcame many significant life and historical challenges to become one of the most prominent and respected scientists of his time. Carver said, "Where there is no vision, there is no hope" (History.com, 2023).

Without a clear vision, people feel lost, even aimless. Within a sea of more possibilities than ever before, it's impossible to choose and stick to a course without a clear idea of where you ultimately want to go. When you have a vision, it becomes a rudder helping you stay the course of the overall direction of your life. A strong vision helps you make decisions, like how to spend your time, the habits you focus on creating, and even the relationships (like friendships) you make or let go of (Logan, n.d.).

> When you have a vision, it becomes a rudder helping you stay the course of the overall direction of your life.

Far more than just a wish list about material possessions, money, and career, a *vision* should describe the many aspects of life an individual dreams for. In fact, the most sustaining visions are not attachments to specifics, but are descriptions of *values* made clear through describing a picture of a reality worth working toward. A vision can serve as something of great value that makes it worthwhile for a hero to continually face the dragons of life. But oddly, the vision itself can be scary. This is because if you dream about something you really care about it and don't achieve it, it hurts. In that way, you become your own judge, learning and refining with each attempt. It's like creating your own dragon to face. So learners often need a little courage to get started.

## More of Cody's Story

I pulled Cody back into my office. I had replayed in my mind numerous times the conversation he and I had the week before (see page 5). The moment was seared in my memory when he pointed at me and through clenched teeth and hissed, "What does it matter? 'Cause I'm never gettin' outta here!"

He was calm this time as I sat across from him at a small table. I offered him a piece of candy from a jar, as well as some reassurance: "You're not in trouble. I just wanted to talk with you. Is that OK?"

He replied with a typical easygoing shrug, "OK."

I told him I didn't feel good about our conversation a week or so ago. He nodded more seriously, remembering the moment now too. I dove right in. "Cody, what do you want your life to be like?" He looked confused. I went on, "You know, like in the future. If you could wave a magic wand, what would you really want your life to be like?"

He nodded his head, now understanding what I was asking. He opened up right away because he trusted me (and our relationship). Cody said, "Mr. Hansen, I don't want my family to be like *my* family."

I nodded, thinking I knew what he meant. I clarified, "But, you want to have a family? Children?"

"Yeah," he said. He wanted to be married and have two boys. I asked more questions about this ideal future. I listened intently as he painted a picture that became beautiful with vibrant details about his future relationships. It was touching to see this tough student talk about being a dad.

Out of the blue, he said he wanted to coach Little League Baseball. I nodded, not letting him know how emotionally caught off guard I was. I knew Cody had never played on a Little League team. But he wanted to be a good dad and a good influence for others too. He wanted to give back to his community—a community that arguably had given him little! I managed a husky, "That's good, Cody. That's good." It was a serious talk. I knew it, and he knew it. After he answered all my questions, describing family dinners and vacations, coaching Little League games, going for ice cream after games, and putting his kids to bed, we sat silent, enveloped in the tangible glow of Cody's description of his ideal future. It was simple, calm, and beautiful.

Surprised by my emotion, I blurted, "But Cody, you've got to make money to support your family. What's your plan? How are you going to make money? If you could wave your magic wand, what would you want to do for work?"

He said he wanted to be a demolition man. I shrugged, not trying to guess the psychology there, and said, "OK, so do you want to be the guy running the shovel with a wooden handle or the guy who's running the heavy equipment shovel?" He made the motions of moving levers for heavy equipment, "I want to run the big shovel." By now I had handed him a blank piece of paper, and he had been writing the details of his vision.

I grabbed my laptop, and we looked up some technical colleges where he could learn how to operate, do maintenance on, and even fix heavy equipment. Cody wrote down the name of the technical school and the cost of tuition.

I asked where he was going to live. Did he want to live in an apartment or a house? "I want to live in a motor home!" he smiled. I didn't question it, we just looked it up. (Those things are expensive!)

"Are you going to have a car or drive your motor home to the worksite? Cell phone? Vacation?" By this time, his blank paper was nearly full of handwritten notes with details of his ideal future, his dream. We printed pages full of resources to support his vision.

Finally, I paused. Slowly, but deliberately I took the paper from him. I looked at it for a good long while. Cody was watching me nod, perhaps a bit anxious for approval and nervous about potential rejection. I turned the paper back around and slid it back in front of him and then tapped it hard repeatedly with my finger, drawing his gaze back to what used to be a blank piece of paper, now made priceless by his vision. I said with a fierceness that surprised me and him, "Cody, do you realize, *this* could be yours?"

He looked at the paper and just stared at it. It was like it was the first time he'd ever allowed himself to really consider his future. After a long moment, he nodded his head almost imperceptibly at first and then he looked up, staring me right in the eyes, but this time, without the anger, hopelessness, frustration, or despair from a week before.

Then with an intensity that snuck up on me again, I said, "But, Cody, you've got to do some things to get there, man! You know what you've gotta do?"

"I've got to graduate from that tech school."

I replied quickly, "Yeah, and before that?"

"I got to get through middle school, high school?"

"And before that?

"I gotta get through math intervention."

"Yeah Cody, you do! I know you can, Cody. I know it! I think you trust me, and I think you know I wouldn't lie to you."

He nodded, and carefully folded up his piece of paper and slid it into his pocket. With no more words between us, I gave him another piece of candy and sent him on his way.

After this conversation with Cody, I met with the mathematics intervention team. We lamented over our frustration of feeling like we were pulling teeth by forcing compliance, and students were not taking ownership of their learning. We redesigned our mathematics intervention classes to better mirror the principles in this book. We blew up our award-winning system and started over, in part because of Cody and so many learners like him. We needed students to start taking ownership of their learning and their future. We couldn't force students to learn at the rigor levels they needed to, and we were going to burn out trying unless they started to own the learning too.

We failed forward, not knowing exactly what we were doing. However, we were learning and helping more students learn the essential academic skills, but more importantly, we were helping them change their story.

Cody had been in mathematics intervention for over two years—two years of reinforcing evidence of his fixed-minded story! After the redesign of mathematics intervention and Cody's creation of his vision, it only took six weeks before Cody worked his way out of mathematics intervention. He passed the state assessment, but that's not the best part of Cody's story.

I pulled Cody into my office on the last day of school to chat and say goodbye, as he was moving up to high school. I also wanted to maybe give him one last pep talk. I started, "It's been a while since we visited."

"Yeah, Mr. Hansen, I've been doing good. I haven't been in here for a long time." We both smiled. Cody said "Hey, you know I passed my state math test this year and I got out of math intervention?"

"Yeah! I know, Cody. I was the guy who handed you that certificate of recognition when you passed, remember?"

"Oh, yeah," he smiled back. I nodded, knowing he remembered. He just wanted a little more validation and recognition. I was happy to give it. He'd earned it.

I got serious and leaned forward, "Do you remember that conversation we had months ago? The one where we sat right here and we talked about your future and your dreams?"

Cody nodded as he said, "Yeah, I remember."

It was then that I asked the question I had been thinking about and wanted to ask him in this last one-to-one conversation. "Cody, are your dreams still the same?"

He didn't speak. Instead, he quietly fished out his wallet. Confused, I watched patiently as he opened the wallet and reached into where the bills were supposed to go. It didn't escape me that there weren't any bills. In fact, the *only* thing in his wallet was one folded piece of paper. Carefully, he pulled it out, unfolded it, and smoothed it out on the table, exactly where he had created it. Tattered and worn on the edges, it was the same piece of paper he had used months ago as he painted that beautiful vision of his ideal future. He looked up solemnly, with hopeful eyes, and said, "Yeah, Mr. Hansen. My dreams are still the same." I nodded for a good while. I couldn't speak.

When I found my voice, I looked him right in the eyes and spoke, "You need to understand something, Cody!"

It came tumbling out in a rush. "I have never lied to you. Not once! And I won't do it now. I need you to know something . . . I believe in you! And you better not let me down! Do you understand me?"

He met my stare and then he nodded. I nodded too. We were silent. There was nothing left to say. We sat awkwardly for a moment, perhaps just letting the silence be a witness of this temporary moment in time when two stories intersected. Finally, I stood up. I stuck out my hand to shake his and tell him goodbye. He rushed past my hand and gave me a hug instead.

As he headed out the door Cody said, "Mr. Hansen, thanks for caring about me and thanks for believing in me." I silently nodded as he left.

## All Students Need a Vision

I hesitated to write Cody's story. I didn't want you to mistakenly think this story was about me. The experience with Cody is part of my journey, for sure. I will be forever grateful for Cody and his influence on my life. *But it's Cody's story: he's the hero.* I chose to tell this part of his story to show how much students need a vision for their future, especially students who come from challenging home environments or who have no natural or inherent models in their lives at home (Bandura, 1997).

Bandura (1977) explains that one of the key ways a student can develop efficacy beliefs (or hold hope about the future) is to have models. In other words, if students have someone who looks like them or came from similar circumstances and has achieved a valued goal, they can potentially see themselves in that person and think, "If he can do it, maybe I can too." Bandura (1997) calls it "vicarious experience" (p. 86). Many students have these role models in their lives (part of their family or other support structures), but many students don't. Educators should try to help provide such role models. Sadly, those opportunities are often limited. There just aren't enough Big Brother or Big Sister programs (or similar programs) to support students who lack hope and the influence of a positive role model.

Thankfully, there's another way. Bandura (1997) explains what he calls "mastery experiences," which are even more powerful at developing efficacy beliefs in an individual than having a model (p. 80). *Mastery experiences* are involvements where a student strives toward a goal, has success, and then recognizes that success is a result of the student's efforts. With enough mastery experiences, students can overcome the need for a role model, especially when those experiences are part of an articulated vision. If educators can help students find a vision and a role model, great! But students can have success without the vicarious experience a role model provides; students can achieve a vision if they believe in it and feel the success of their progress toward it.

Adding confirmatory evidence to Bandura's (1997) findings for why mastery experiences *feel* good are deeper understandings of the neurochemical source dopamine (Huberman, 2022). But dopamine isn't serving to just provide a transient reward; it is reinforcing the preceding behavior, essentially telling the brain to do the behavior again. If the repeated behavior leads to further progress toward a desirable goal, the brain releases more dopamine again, creating sort of a reinforcing loop. If a learner stays consistent, they form habits, thus changing the physical neuropathways of the brain itself (Huberman, 2022). This is why video games are so addictive. There is a clear vision (or quest) and the games are designed to reward the players with small dopaminergic rewards through the incremental progress of passing levels. Many students just need a real-life vision to work toward instead of an artificial one.

In the absence of natural role models, educators must help students (especially those who've had more challenging past experiences in school and at home) intentionally craft their vision and help them *believe* it's possible to achieve. Learners need mastery experiences of moving toward the goal, but they are more likely to believe in a vision (especially at first) if someone they trust and respect believes in it too—regardless of whether that trusted adult looks like them or comes from where they come from. In the following sections, I'll discuss why a vision is so powerful, what should be in a vision, and how your relationship with students will breathe life into their vision.

## A Vision Is Powerful

Simply put, a *vision* is "determining the way you want your life to go" (Robbins, n.d.). With a vision for the ideal future, students' actions in the present can aim with intention at that future. The journeyers have a destination they can move toward.

An articulated vision also provides a way to assess whether the current actions of journeyers are bringing them closer to or further from their vision. You can see if you and
your actions align toward your ideal, but only if you have articulated your ideal. Rogers
(1961) believes striving toward alignment is not only a means
to accomplish the desired future but also a fundamental and
innate human need to simply strive toward something.
Without a vision, people feel lost and can lack hope.

*Without a vision,
people feel lost.*

People have a need to strive toward an ideal, but it's clear that fulfillment isn't actually
in the eventual accomplishment, but in the *striving* (Huberman, 2022). It's a tired trope,
but true nonetheless, that *happiness is found in the journey, not the destination*. Those who
learn to bring their current actions into alignment with their ideal future experience a
much greater satisfaction, sense of purpose, and wholeness in life (Rogers, 1961). The outcome of alignment is a mental state of purposeful action, while simultaneously enjoying
a sense of inner peace and confidence. Sounds pretty great, right?

Think about the importance of alignment for a moment. How powerful would it be
if your child and all the students in the school learned how to craft a vision and then
self-assess (if their current actions align to bringing their vision into fruition) as part
of the essential curriculum? What kind of a difference would that make for the social,
emotional, and academic well-being of students? This is no small thing! The implication
and overall benefit would be massive for students. There are some questions later in this
chapter to help you guide students through such a self-assessment (see page 97). But first,
read more about what a vision should look like and how to get there.

## Crafting the Vision

A vision should include more than just what job students want, the type of car they
want to drive, and whether they want to be able to fly first class. The vision should
articulate ideal circumstances of family, job, relationships, and *who* the student aims
to become. Many school-based social-emotional learning programs help students plan
out their academic and career future, but usually don't help students go much deeper.
Schools or teachers often shy away from envisioning more than just future jobs because
they fear potential parent accusations that the teacher or school is trying to impose their
personal values on students. Teachers need to be sensitive to the fact that ideas about the
ideal are as diverse as the students themselves and the cultures from which they come.
But my experience is that simply letting parents know your intentions, explaining that
students each will be self-directing their vision creation, then sharing any materials they

use in the discussions, and letting parents know they can simply ask you if they have any questions, easily mitigates this concern.

It's important to help students craft a *holistic vision* for their future, not just about their future career. While work is an important part of people's lives, it is far from being everything. For many students, it's overwhelming to think about a future job or career. Students often feel pressure to decide right then, but it's much easier and actually fun to craft a vision about a future life and name the things you know you want. They get to dream a bit. Besides, jobs and even careers will come and go.

What other things might students include in their vision? I don't think there are "right" or "wrong" answers here. The more personal the vision, the better. Some students will need more support than others when thinking about the life they want to describe. Considerations will also vary depending on the environment and age of the students. Don't underestimate how young students can start to articulate a vision. But first, what matters to *you?* Knowing what you know, because of the hard-earned wisdom of a life lived so far, what would you want in your vision for the future besides your future job? These sorts of questions can help inform what questions may have helped you on your journey.

## Questions to Ask

There isn't one way or format for articulating this vision. Just start with a blank piece of paper. I've seen students simply write about the future like they were writing a journal entry. I've seen bullet points, word clouds, free verse poetry, and even drawings. Questions should be age appropriate, but following are a few prompts that might help you help learners get started if they are struggling. These prompts are not meant as a worksheet for learners to fill out, but as a resource for informing their thinking. Visit **go.SolutionTree.com/instruction** for a free reproducible version of this list.

» Relationships

  » What will your future important relationships look and feel like? You might consider a partner, kids, family, friends, coworkers, and others.

  » What qualities are important to you in those relationships? Examples include honesty, trust, care, and loyalty.

  » How will you maintain healthy and positive connections with those you have a relationship with?

» What traditions would you like to continue from your current family? What would you like to change?

» Recreation and leisure

  » What are some hobbies that bring you joy now? How do you see yourself incorporating these hobbies in the future?

  » What new hobbies do you want to learn?

  » Are there special places you want to go or specific adventures you want to experience?

  » How do you see yourself relaxing and rejuvenating? What practices help you recharge?

» Community

  » What is something you wish could change in your community? How will your future self help solve this problem?

  » What kind of impact would you like to have in your community? In the world?

» Nature

  » What is your connection with nature like now?

  » How do you picture your connection with nature in future?

» Physical, mental, and emotional well-being

  » What exercise and fitness levels do you want to attain in the future? How do you see yourself staying active and healthy?

  » What practices do you envision yourself using to manage stress and stay emotionally present?

  » How will you continue to learn and grow?

  » What skills or knowledge would you like to learn?

» Finances and lifestyle

  » How will you manage your finances to ensure stability and security?

  » Can you picture a future of *financial freedom* (the freedom to pursue your interests and passions without financial constraints)?

  » Are you going to have pets? What kind?

» What kind of lifestyle do want to have in the future? Examples include rural, urban, home, apartment, simple, and extravagant.

» Where might you live?

» Work

» Do you like working with other people or on your own?

» What are some things you are good at or enjoy doing?

» What are you interested in learning more about?

» How do you envision your work aligning with your passions and values?

» Do you know what kind of job or career you want?

» How will you create a work-life balance?

» Spiritual well-being (optional)

» What practices contribute to your well-being and sense of purpose?

» What practices do you envision having in the future?

» What other parts of your life would you like to describe?

Prompts such as these will help students start crafting their vision. The more they own their vision and the process for creating it, the better, but it's helpful for them to envision as many facets of their future as is developmentally appropriate.

## Backmapping the Journey

Once students have thought through these or other prompts, have them complete a *backmapping your journey handout.* This tool makes the vision more than just a dream; it helps students start to plan out the steps they can take now to start moving toward their vision. Together, the vision and the beginning of a plan to get there helps provide purpose in students' daily efforts. Figure 6.1 (page 100) shows an example completed version of the backmapping handout. This tool allows students to backmap their plan for reaching their vision by starting with the vision, then working backward until they get to the steps they can currently be taking to achieve their vision.

Remy, grade 6

**Your Vision!**

Write a few words or draw a small picture that represents your vision of the future here.

* Start animal shelter
* Coach soccer
* Married 2-3 kids
* Family trips with cousins
* Live by beach
* 2 dogs, 1 cat, and a raccoon named Bandit

**Next steps:**

* Veterinary school
* Get engaged
* Volunteer soccer coach

**Next steps:**

* College (biology and business)
* Work at an animal shelter
* Good friends, boyfriend

**Next steps:**

* High school
* Volunteer at animal shelter
* Get better at talking to people
* Get good grades. Maybe scholarship?

**You are here!**

Name three steps you can take right now to move you closer to your vision.

1. Watch videos online to learn about animal shelters

2. Say "hi" to the people I sit by in class

3. Get better at math

**FIGURE 6.1:** Example of backmapping the journey.

*Visit **go.SolutionTree.com/instruction** for a free blank reproducible version of this figure.*

## Reviewing the Vision

Students' visions for their future jobs, where they want to live, and other details will likely change many times as the students mature, have life experiences, discover their strengths and passions, and take on responsibility. That's OK, and students need to know it's OK too. It's not important they achieve their exact vision; it's important that they're working toward something, even if that something changes many times. Some of the core values students articulate by describing what they desire in things like relationships with people, nature, and their community will often stay the same, acting as a consistent rudder in a sea of possibilities of many transient things like jobs, hobbies, and location. Even if big changes occur, it doesn't matter. Simply by working toward something, students are learning how to articulate what they want, how to plan, and then take steps toward getting it. This is vital for students to become the hero in their own story and journey. Despite transforming into people much more capable, learners still may not ever reach their vision. But by articulating it and working toward their vision, students are at least moving toward the best version of themselves they can currently see.

It's important to be honest as you communicate with your learners, letting them know that life always throws everyone a few surprises—some more than others. People don't always get what they want, even when they are clear and work really hard. I think it's just as important to help learners understand that even if life throws you a curve and you don't get what you intended, working hard toward a vision still puts you in the best possible situation to have good things happen, even if not exactly what you intended. Trusting that your effort will pay off— even if not a hundred percent the way you want— is an indication of a person with high self-efficacy. The more students feel compelled toward their future vision, the more trust they will have in it, their actions toward it, and the goodness of unanticipated results. A clear vision is a powerful thing!

> *Trusting that your effort will pay off— even if not a hundred percent the way you want—is an indication of a person with high self-efficacy.*

To access the full power of a vision, students should review theirs regularly. Occasionally ask students, individually or in large groups, to review their vision and backmap. Ask students questions like the following.

» "Has your vision changed or do you want to add more details to it?"

» "How well have you been executing your plan?"

» "What level of effort have you been giving?"

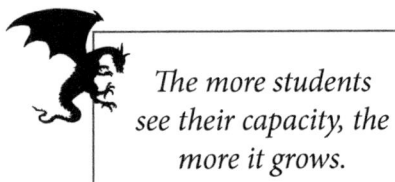

*The more students see their capacity, the more it grows.*

» "What's one thing you can you do today to help bring yourself into better alignment with your vision?"

By periodically helping learners review their vision, self-assess, make corrections, and celebrate successes, teachers are helping them see their capacity to work and make progress toward a vision. The more students see their capacity, the more it grows.

## Concluding Thoughts

In chapter 2 (page 35), I covered the importance of not only creating a relationship of trust but also leveraging it to help learners take a step toward the unknown of their potential. It's an important part of the Hero-Maker Framework. A relationship of trust also provides a powerful opportunity for helping a learner not just create a vision, but *believe* in it.

If you follow the Hero-Maker Framework in this book, you will help your learners start to see themselves differently through new experiences. Students will see they are more capable than they might have previously thought, and also see that you are capable too. Learners will trust that what you say will happen actually happens, precisely because it has before. Teachers rarely see themselves this way, but to your learners, you are wise. It's almost as if you can predict the future, like a wizard!

Now, put yourself in the place of one of your learners. Imagine you have a powerful person in your life and this person sits you down and helps you map out a vision. After investing some precious time with you on that vision, the person tells you with trustworthy conviction and sincerity, "I believe in your vision." It's clear the person truthfully believes you can accomplish it. It doesn't matter that you may not look like the person or come from the same place; because that powerful, trustworthy person believes in your vision, you begin to have the courage to believe in it too.

I vividly remember a conversation about the principles of trust and belief with a principal I was supporting and coaching. Very vulnerably, she told me her story. The principal explained how she had been raised in an abusive home environment. She got herself and her younger siblings to school, although often wearing dirty clothes and unprepared. She was at best a middle-of-the-road student (nothing special), until one wizardly teacher intervened. With a year's worth of wizardly credibility built, on the very last day of middle school, this teacher gifted her a yearbook, knowing she likely didn't have the money to buy one. In it, the teacher scribed an encouraging note to this fourteen-year-old learner, ending with this sentence: "You are going to be the valedictorian of your class, and I will be there to cheer!" Yes, you guessed it, this young girl from an abusive home made it her vision to become the valedictorian and did. I relay this story not to promote *giving* students a vision. It's better if students develop their own, but the story illustrates the power your belief in students and their vision can have on them.

I encourage you to sit with your students and be available for them to have some of these conversations. Some learners may not need courage from you. Others might desperately need it. Your attention and words will breathe life into their vision. If you just don't have the time to have this kind of conversation with each of your learners, then prioritize which students need courage the most.

What really matters here is not what's in the vision (that is, what categories students cover or whether their vision is even feasible or completely realistic). Creating a vision is simply setting an intention, not trying to control everything. Life is like a puzzle, not a game of chess. People take what comes, accept it, and move forward. This exercise is not about mapping out every step learners must take. It's about helping motivate students to take action and getting them to see that by aiming at one thing, their lives will be better, even though it's almost inevitable that life will turn out differently than what they envision. That's OK. Help learners set their intentions and let go of the exact results, trusting good will come from following the hero's path.

# CHAPTER 7

# Hero-Maker Framework Tools

This chapter is different from the six previous chapters. It's the technical, how-to instructions for work teachers or teacher teams do to implement the Hero-Maker Framework. This chapter shows you how to quickly develop the tools you need.

The intention of this chapter is to help you avoid getting stuck in endless planning purgatory. There's just enough to get you started on the intentional work of developing efficacy, using one essential academic skill of your choosing as the medium. The experience of working your way all the way through the process with one skill will serve as a guide for continuing the work of developing self-efficacy with your learners through other skills in the future. In many cases, teams will do this work (which is ideal), but I will speak to individual teachers. Just know all these concepts are just as applicable for collaborative teams as they are for individual teachers.

The tasks I outline are necessary to create the tools you'll need to follow the Hero-Maker Framework with your learners. Following are the five tasks covered in this chapter.

1. Identify *essential skills* and choose one to focus on in an upcoming unit.

2. Create a *model of proficiency*.

3. Create a *description of quality* that describes why the models are proficient.

4. Anticipate and name the *typical pitfalls* students will encounter on the path to proficiency.

5. Develop *progress trackers* for teachers and learners.

Accomplishing these tasks, which can be done quickly, will lead to the creation of the tools you need to begin implementing the framework. I'll explain each tool and how to develop each tool. Much of this will feel familiar to teachers because they have done so much of this kind of work in the past. In the past, however, teachers did the work in service of different aims. This time, teachers are doing this work not just to help students learn academic skills but also in service of their own purpose of helping learners become heroes on their own learning journey, story, and life. You are doing this work to intentionally develop self-efficacy in learners.

In addition to giving instructions for how to develop the tools, I'll make a few additions to the knowledge base you've already gained from the other chapters about how to *use* the tools. I'll discuss how teachers should think differently about the educational tools or concepts than they traditionally have. Some tools will look and feel familiar, but teachers must unlearn some of their previous assumptions and experiences to make room for relearning their new purpose. That's hard. I encourage you to intentionally follow the steps your first time with a beginner's mindset. Try to think about the tools from the perspective of your new purpose, not your old experience. Don't just use the old tools you used in the past. Teachers must let the old concepts die to make room for new growth, just like the mythological phoenix in so many stories; the phoenix burns, but is reborn out of the ashes into something new, more glorious, powerful, and beautiful.

Let's get started.

## Identify Essential Skills

Chapter 1 (page 19) explains how important it is for both for teachers and students to understand learning goals. Before communicating learning goals, teachers must choose and articulate the essential academic skills. The problem is, most content teachers who are passionate about their subject can make a case that just about every standard is essential. The result is a list of too many essentials. I regularly hear from teachers who express the dissonance they feel knowing there is too much to cover when they say something like, "Even though we have developed essentials, there still isn't enough time to teach them all, let alone provide intervention. So even though we want to, how would we even attempt to do the kind of deep empowerment work and self-efficacy development you're talking about?" I get it! There is so much to cover! These good-hearted professionals are trying so hard to do what their schools expect of them. They don't know it, but they (like so many of their students) are acting out of compliance or pleasing others. If teachers don't see their own compliant behaviors, they will never empower others to break free from the chains of compliance.

If there is still too much to cover after determining your essentials, ask yourself, "What are the essentials of the essentials? What *really* matters for students' futures?" Not all standards are equally important, and teachers must prioritize which skills are going to best equip students with the skills they really need to claim their space and compete in an ever-changing world. In the limited time you have for intervention, for which of these skills are you going to provide intense intervention? What's worth your limited time? Prioritizing becomes a little more doable with these new constraints on the decisions, as is recognizing time is finite and constant. Just because you don't deem a standard essential doesn't mean it's not important and you won't teach it. Teachers must identify the academic skills worthy of a hero's effort, which they will use to do the deeper work of the Hero-Maker Framework: helping students develop self-efficacy.

Choosing what's essential also gives teachers permission to take the time students need to develop skills that really matter on a deep level (Conley, 2010). If needed, do a quick review of chapter 3 (page 47) to help prime your decisions. For primary grades, the essentials of foundational literacy and numeracy skills you've always considered essential should still be at the top of your list, but you should be including deeper-thinking skills too.

## Create Version 1.0 of Your Essentials

So, what are the essentials of your essentials? What are the skills that really matter for your students? Make a short list and label it "Essentials Version 1.0, DRAFT," and add the date at the top. This gives you permission to change it later, as you most certainly will for versions 2.0, 3.0, and so on. This is a working document! Set a date for when you'll revisit your list and make revisions. Following is some guidance to help you take a step toward version 1.0 and get started using the framework. Figure 7.1 (page 108) shows an example of an essentials list.

*Ninth-Grade English Language Arts Essentials Version 1.0, Draft Date: April 16*

» **Research skills:** *Use tools strategically to find, evaluate, and use information from various sources to become informed about an issue.*

» **Critical-reading skills:** *Comprehend and evaluate grade-level texts, identifying main ideas, analyzing arguments, and drawing evidence-based conclusions.*

» **Writing arguments:** *Make and write arguments to support claims with clear reasons and relevant evidence.*

» **Empathy:** *Demonstrate an ability to understand multiple points of view on an issue and what would be compelling to a potential audience.*

» **Collaboration:** *Work effectively in diverse teams by collaborating with others and respecting different viewpoints to achieve shared goals.*

**FIGURE 7.1:** Example of an essentials version 1.0 list.

1. **Look at your course standards and determine which skills *really* matter for students:** Essential skills matter for students' success in future schooling opportunities and life.

2. **Make your essentials list:** Don't overthink it. Write down a few skills you are confident are essential. You can include more later. Teams often set a time limit of no more than twenty minutes for the discussion, and members remind one another this is just a first draft.

3. **Set a date for future review and revision of your list:** Revise regularly as you continue to learn. Your list will grow as you get better and more efficient at using the framework.

Next, you'll need to choose one essential from your list to work on.

## Choose One Essential to Get Started

Looking at your list of essentials, choose an essential skill and use the Hero-Maker Framework to focus on that essential skill during an upcoming unit. Following are a few prompts to help your decision making.

1. If you could wave your magic wand, what's one gift or academic skill you'd really like to give your students in the next few weeks during the upcoming unit?

2. Does this skill really matter for students' success in both school and life? Will the skill help them contend in the world?

3. Is this skill worth using your precious intervention time on?

For example, say you start with the skill *Write arguments to support claims with clear reasons and relevant evidence.* If a student can do this, the student can attend and graduate from college. I would argue it's an *essential of the essentials*, regardless of the student's chosen vocation.

The content varies depending on the class and grade level. In science, students might argue with evidence to support their hypotheses about mitosis, while students in social studies might argue for an amendment to the constitution. Students in auto tech may argue their diagnosis of mechanical problems and support their claim with evidence. The content doesn't matter so much, as long as it's engaging; the essential skill is the focus. Regardless, every teacher and content, grade-level, and interdisciplinary team will choose specific skills all can agree are absolutely the essentials of the essentials. Choose one essential that really matters for your students' futures and is worthy of your efforts and the efforts of would-be heroes to start the Hero-Maker Framework process.

## Create a Model of Proficiency

Next, decide on a model (or models) of proficiency. Even after you identify your version 1.0 essentials, it's common to still be unclear about what you actually want students to learn or at what level of rigor you want them to learn it. The process for gathering or creating models is simple. If you've already started working on this particular skill (or have in the past), you can pull examples of student work you think show what proficiency on the essential skill looks like.

If you're working in a team and each member brings samples of student work, invariably, someone brings a sample that's beyond proficient (or a mastery-level example), and someone else brings a sample that's not quite at the level the team thinks is proficient. Through conversations, members come to consensus on a model at the proficient level. Through your conversations about the different samples, you'll start creating *inter-rater reliability*, which simply means you have enough discussion with other members to basically agree on the different levels of performance students must achieve to be considered proficient. This is an important step in creating an equitable grading system, but it's deeper than that (Guskey, 2015). It's a step toward creating equitable learning expectations, or what Marzano (2003) calls *a guaranteed and viable curriculum.*

If you don't have ready access to student work from which to pull models, take twenty minutes and create your own. Pretend to be one of your sixth graders, first graders, or tenth graders, and write a response or create some other piece of work (depending on the essential skill your students are working on) at the rigor level you think students should be able to perform to be considered proficient.

Once you decide on a model, label it "Model of Proficiency Version 1.0, DRAFT" and add the date at the top, just as we did for the working draft of the list of essentials. Figure 7.2 shows an example of a model of proficiency. Note that later, after identifying targets, you may come back to the model of proficiency to color-code the targets that are embedded (highlighting different targets in different colors). Doing so can be helpful to further illuminate the learning goal for students and help them self-assess their work against the model.

---

*Eighth-Grade English Language Arts Model of Proficiency Version 1.0, Draft Date: April 2*

*Write arguments to support claims with clear reasons and relevant evidence.*

*In the book To Kill a Mockingbird, one of the themes is about what it means to have courage. Atticus teaches his son that courage isn't about physical strength or being tough, but about doing the right thing for the right reason, even if it's hard. (1) While talking to his son, he tries to explain what courage is: "It's knowing you're licked before you begin but you begin anyway and you see it through no matter what. You rarely win, but sometimes you do." (2) Atticus also shows his kids that he means what he says because he continues to defend Tom Robison in court, even though he's destined to lose. Atticus knows this but he doesn't quit. He keeps trying even though it's hard and there might even be some harsh consequences for doing the right thing. Atticus doesn't just talk about courage. He shows the world that he actually has courage because he does the right thing no matter what, even when it's hard.*

---

*Source: Adapted from Lee, 1960.*

**FIGURE 7.2:** Example of a model of proficiency.

Anytime you decide, you can change, tweak, add to, or replace the model as you get clearer about what it is you want your students to learn and consistently do to demonstrate they've learned the essential. Vet your model later against released items from the state assessment or ask for trusted colleagues' opinions. This is wise to ensure your rigor expectations are on par with others' expectations. Over time, you'll end up with multiple models of proficiency you and your learners can use. But for now, *done is better than perfect.*

Models of proficiency are as varied as the skills they represent. In woodshop, if the overarching intended learning goal is to acquire the skills needed to build simple furniture, the teacher might present a model nightstand to help show learners the specific subset of skills necessary to be proficient overall. If a science class is working on interpreting a data set to make a hypothesis, the model could be a month's worth of moon phase data with a properly formulated hypothesis about a moon phase on a particular date in the future. In mathematics, teachers have always used models of proficiency to show students how to work algorithms. Models become even more useful when students are learning more rigorous skills, such as real-world problem solving. A model for the skill of calculating area in the real world might be an example of how one former student calculated the area for a sprinkler system design.

The bottom line is to get clear about what academic skills you *really* want students to learn. Then find or create examples of what proficient performance actually looks like on that skill. Share those samples with students to help them get clear about what proficiency looks like on the skill too.

## Create Descriptions of Quality

The intention with this next step is to help illuminate even more what the learning goal is. Think about it this way: imagine you have never eaten a soufflé in your life, nor do you even know what one looks like. It would be difficult to make one, right? Seeing and tasting a model soufflé would super helpful. Even more helpful would be if your instructor explained the elements of a good soufflé as you looked at and sampled a model together. This is what *descriptions of quality* do; they explain *why* the models are quality work. But the description of a quality soufflé won't help you get really clear about making a soufflé if you haven't seen one first. That's why you start with a model.

It's worth noting here that some learning is generally rote development of discrete knowledge or skills and, therefore, does not lend itself to the development of descriptions of quality. Some skills or knowledge you either have or you don't. For example, in the lower elementary grades, you may choose to help your learners take ownership of learning letter sounds. Descriptions of what quality work looks like aren't going to really help add clarity for the learner. This isn't to say learning letter sounds isn't worthy of a young hero's effort. It most certainly is, and you can easily use learning letter sounds for the dual purpose of developing self-efficacy!

Start creating your descriptions of quality by simply describing a few reasons *why* the models of proficient work are actually proficient. In other words, describe a few essential things a learner has to do consistently to be considered proficient at making soufflés, building furniture, writing an argumentative claim, welding a pipe, and so on. You might be wondering at this point, "Wait, aren't you just talking about rubrics?" Yes, but I don't like using that term at first. There are a number of reasons I don't, including the tendency teachers have to think they can skip the step of creating their own rubrics. Teachers usually turn to a search engine or teacher-sharing websites and look for work others have already done. The problem with doing this is that many rubrics are so convoluted, long, and wordy they don't add clarity for students. Also, because the rubrics are not connected to models, they can actually make the learning goal even more unclear. Teachers don't own what they don't create.

So instead, ask yourself with your new model of proficiency in front of you, "What makes this quality work? Why is this proficient work?" List four or five important things the model does. It's that simple! That's really all a rubric is—a description of why something is quality. Usually, a rubric will give gradient values to help teachers indicate the degree to which those descriptions of quality are present in students' work. You can do that later if you want, but for now, keep things simple.

It's efficient for teachers to start with models of proficient work and clearly describe what characteristics of the models make them quality work. The rubric is clear because it points right back to the model. Following the same pattern, teachers will be able to communicate with their learners by helping those learners first experience the soufflé and then clarifying even more by using the rubric to discuss the soufflé. Another benefit of developing the rubric yourself instead of just searching for one online is *you will own it*. Label your work "Description of Quality Version 1.0, DRAFT" and add the date. Figure 7.3 shows an example of a description of quality.

---

*Description of Quality Version 1.0, Draft Date: April 16*

*Write arguments to support claims with a clear reason and relevant evidence.*

» *A clear claim is made. It's logical and shows a clear understanding and interpretation of the text.*

» *The evidence makes sense and is credible. The explanation, along with evidence, logically supports the claim.*

» *The evidence is cited properly and is smoothly integrated in the text. (For example: The author states, _____.)*

» *A concluding statement wraps things up, reiterating the point.*

---

**FIGURE 7.3**: Example of a description of quality version 1.0 list.

Remember as you create, done is better than perfect—having clear and effective ways for communicating the learning goal is what you're after, not perfect products.

# Anticipate Pitfalls on the Path to Proficiency

The task of *anticipating pitfalls* will help you make the shift from directed to facilitated feedback, like I discuss in chapter 4 (page 63). Making this shift will help students begin to self-assess and track their progress. Without this step, learners won't be able to accurately track their progress, know what they need to work on, or engage in the metacognitive reflection they need to intentionally build self-efficacy. What's important is that learners can see their progress over time. The progress needs to be specific. So how do you track progress?

## Track Progress

Sometimes learning happens sequentially, and it's nice when it does. Educators teach step one, step two, step three, and so on. If all goes as planned, the learning of each step leads to proficiency of the overarching skill or intended learning goal. In that case, it seems simple; teachers can track the learning of each step. Yes, it's sometimes that simple! For example, learning letter sounds is essential for kindergartners. Teachers may help these learners track mastery of their letter sounds one letter at a time as a step toward reaching the overarching goal of knowing all the letter sounds. Some teachers may group letters together as tracked steps (A–E, F–J, and so on). Some learners may need more time on certain steps, but it is relatively simple to track their progress. The problem is that learning is often much more organic than step-by-step teaching and students just "getting it," especially as the learning becomes more rigorous.

Despite inherently knowing this, many educators are stuck in a teaching-centric mindset. It shows up when teachers follow a strictly adhered to and sequenced schedule of lessons. Inherent in the reluctance to deviate from the schedule is an abdication of the teachers' responsibility for learning: "I taught what I was supposed to teach. It's not my fault they didn't learn it."

Because of this, as teachers develop their skills as leaders of learning, they spend more energy on formatively assessing than they do on teaching the lessons. They become more *learning-centric* than teaching-centric. In other words, if learning is a journey, good teachers want to know which *pitfalls* each learner may fall into on the path to proficiency. The reason teachers want this information in real time is because if they know what is tripping up each learner, they still have a chance to provide the help each learner needs. Wizardly teachers are not just *learning-centric* but *learner-centric*. Through facilitation, the teacher empowers the learners themselves to track their journey and self-select the help they need.

While some learners may struggle on the path to proficiency for some utterly unique reasons, most of the time learners struggle for typical reasons. Drawing on their experience, most teachers can easily anticipate some of the common pitfalls as learners walk the path of learning a particular skill. Identifying typical pitfalls gives teachers clear items to look for and is a lot like giving journeyers a map to help them see where they are (or where they may be stuck) and what is holding them back. So if the learning happens to be a sequential step-by-step process, then the progress of learning each step is likely what you want to track. However, if the learning is more organic, you will likely want to track the pitfalls where learners may get stuck.

Most teachers have experienced the traditional work of unpacking essential standards, and many refer to the sequential steps as *learning targets*. The problem is, after teachers write those targets, they usually view them from a teaching-centric stance or as the targets to teach. In a *teaching-centric stance*, teaching is the job ("If I taught the right things, I did my job."). In a *learning-centric stance*, ensuring students learn the overarching skill is the job. In a *learner-centric stance*, the job is making sure students learn the overarching skill while developing self-efficacy. The more you can think about targets as *pitfalls* you are assessing, the more you are in the mindset to facilitate feedback instead of direct feedback. Whether you label what you're tracking as *targets*, *steps*, or *pitfalls*, doesn't really matter. What's important is you are helping students self-assess, track their progress, and self-select what exactly they still need to work on to continue on the path toward proficiency.

## Create a List of Typical Pitfalls

With this understanding of tracking learning progress, you're ready to name some pitfalls you want to track and also have your learners track on their path to proficiency. For now, don't overthink this; you've likely taught this essential skill before. Draw on that wisdom and ask yourself, "What are the typical pitfalls on the path to proficiency for this overarching skill? Why do students typically struggle?" List three or four things for now. Label your list "Typical Pitfalls Version 1.0, DRAFT" and add the date.

As an example, say you are about to start helping fourth-grade learners tackle adding fractions with unlike denominators. Drawing on wisdom from the past, you might anticipate that one pitfall for some learners will be their conceptual understanding of what a fraction even *is*. They don't understand that one number over another number represents parts of a whole. Another pitfall for some might be the concept of a common denominator. Learners struggling with this pitfall don't understand why they can't just add the numerator with the other numerator and the denominator and the other denominator to get the answer. Some students might conceptualize what they are supposed to do but get lost in the process of solving because they lack fluency in their multiplication facts. Figure 7.4 shows an example of a list of pitfalls for the overarching skill of adding fractions with unlike denominators.

*Typical Pitfalls Version 1.0, Draft Date April 20*

*Add fractions with unlike denominators.*

» *Pitfall one: Some students struggle with conceptual understanding of fractions.*

» *Pitfall two: Some students struggle with the conceptual understanding of a common denominator.*

» *Pitfall three: Some students might know what they are supposed to do but get lost in the process of solving because they lack fluency in multiplication facts.*

**FIGURE 7.4:** Example of a typical pitfalls version 1.0 list.

Often there is strong overlap with the typical pitfalls and descriptions of quality, but they don't always line up exactly, so don't assume they are the same. By naming typical pitfalls, you're trying to predict what students will struggle with on the path. The descriptions of quality help you define what *proficiency looks like*. In the example of adding fractions with unlike denominators, you likely wouldn't create descriptions of quality. The students either got it or didn't, unless your expectation includes the higher levels of rigor of applying adding fractions to solve some real-world problem.

Identifying typical pitfalls is powerful work. If you use them correctly, pitfalls will aid your use of powerful formative assessment practices, facilitated feedback, progress tracking, and aligning specific interventions with students' specific deficits. These pitfalls will also help students accurately assess themselves, track their own progress, and self-determine what specific intervention or practice they need. For your purposes, using pitfalls (or targets) is necessary to empower students because pitfalls give them a map to own their learning journey as heroes.

This is the most complicated, technical part of the Hero-Maker Framework. Don't let yourself get stuck on this by overcomplicating it or trying to get it all exactly right the first time. Start small with two, three, or maybe four pitfalls. Remember, perfection is the enemy of progress. If you've made it this far and are simply trying to move toward facilitated feedback, you are already transforming your practice!

*Perfection is the enemy of progress.*

# Develop Progress Trackers for Teachers and Learners

Creating progress trackers for you and your learners is the last step before you're ready to start the unit of learning.

## Progress Trackers for Teachers

Do the following to create teacher progress trackers.

1. Name the overarching skill students need to learn.

2. Write the names of your students in a column.

3. Using your previously identified typical pitfalls, create pitfall categories with space to record multiple scores over time for each student.

For the teacher's progress tracker, simply take the pitfalls you've identified and put them in a spreadsheet. Since you are already familiar with it, use the progress tracker for teachers from chapter four (see figure 4.1, page 67) as an example. I include it here again for your reference in figure 7.5. The overarching essential skill students are aiming at is *Write arguments to support claims with clear reasons and relevant evidence.* The tracker marks progress toward the overarching skill by tracking some of the targets (or typical pitfalls). Just like when you embark on journey and use a map, you have an overall final destination, but you track your progress on the map as you go. The tracker should include space to record progress on each pitfall multiple times. The simpler, the better. You will use this tool to simply record your observation of your learners' progress as you facilitate feedback with them, like I discuss in chapter 4 (page 63).

| Language Arts Progress Tracker (Teacher) | | | | | | | | | | | | | | | | |
|---|---|---|---|---|---|---|---|---|---|---|---|---|---|---|---|---|
| **Skill:** Write arguments to support claims with clear reasons and relevant evidence. | | | | | | | | | | | | | | | | |
| **Student Names** | **Learning Target 1.a:** Student can make and introduce a logical claim. | | | | **Target 1.b:** Student can support claim with clear reasons and relevant, credible evidence. | | | | **Target 1.c:** Student establishes and maintains formal style. | | | | **Target 1.d:** Student provides a concluding statement. | | | |
| Sarah | 2 | 2 | 3 | 3 | 1 | 1 | 2 | 2 | 2 | 3 | 3 | 4 | | | | |
| Juan | 1 | 2 | 3 | 3 | 1 | 1 | 2 | 2 | 2 | 2 | 3 | 3 | | | | |
| | | | | | | | | | | | | | | | | |
| | | | | | | | | | | | | | | | | |

*Source: Adapted from Hansen, 2015a; White Pine Middle School.*

**FIGURE 7.5:** Example of a teacher's progress tracker.

You may also record any traditional formative assessments like exit tickets or common formative assessments you administer with your team. Remember, these scores aren't for grades (although the benefit of standards-referenced grading becomes pretty obvious when teachers adopt a learning-centric focus and these principles). The scores are simply indications of learners' progress on some of the key concepts they need on the way toward becoming proficient on the overarching skill or learning goal.

Over time, you will see what each learner is still struggling with as the student works toward proficiency. Patterns will also become evident, like when the whole class needs a lesson about a particular pitfall. It will also become evident when a learner is struggling with something that isn't typical, signaling to the teacher this student needs more intensive help. Because some struggles don't always fit into the typical pitfalls, the teacher should sit with the student, try to figure out together what is holding the student back, and determine the next step (specific to the student's ZPD). As teachers get better at transferring ownership, and learners get better at self-assessing and self-directing their improvement, teachers find an unexpected freedom of time to actually (and finally) sit beside the students who need them the most! I regularly hear from teachers about their stress levels going down dramatically when they implement the Hero-Maker Framework, while their students' motivation and learning improves.

When the shift from teaching to learning is complete, the progress tracker becomes more of a preparation guide for the teacher than the traditional lesson plan book or purchased resources. Teachers begin planning by asking themselves, "Who needs what?" not "What am I going to teach today?" It's a liberating stance full of humble confidence.

## Progress Trackers for Learners

Do the following to create student progress trackers.

1. Name the overarching skill learners must learn.

2. List the potential and typical pitfalls and sequential steps (or targets), leaving space for students to record their progress multiple times.

3. Decide on a system where learners will have ready access and extensively use their trackers to track their progress.

Learners' progress trackers are similar to the teacher's (as I discuss in chapter 4, page 63). Students need the same information about the overarching skill and typical pitfalls. Since you are already familiar with it, use the progress tracker for learners (see figure 4.2, page 69) as an example. I include it here again for your reference (see figure 7.6, page 118). Learners each write their name on their tracker and keep it in a safe place. Some teachers keep student trackers in class folders or file crates in the back of the room, or have learners glue it in their notebook. For elementary school learners, some teachers tape it to their desks for students to use daily. Since learners will self-assess using the models of proficiency you share and go over with them, keep the tracker and models of proficiency close. You might even consider putting the tracker on one side of a sheet of paper and a model of proficiency on the other. This will help you refer back to the model as you facilitate feedback and help learners self-discover where they're at and what they need to work on.

| English Language Arts Progress Tracker (Student) | | | | | | |
|---|---|---|---|---|---|---|
| **Name:** Juan Hernandez | | 1 | 2 | 3 | 4 | 5 |
| **Essential Standard** | Write arguments to support claims with clear reasons and relevant evidence. | Date/ Score | Date/ Score | Date/ Score | Date/ Score | Date/ Score |
| **Learning Targets** | This is my progress so far. | Sept 10 | Sept 15 | Sept 22 | Sept 26 | |
| **1.a** | I can make and introduce a logical claim. | 2 | 3 | 3 | 3 | |
| **1.b** | I can support claim with clear reasons and relevant, credible evidence. | 1 | 2 | 2 | 2 | |
| **1.c** | I can establish and maintain formal style (including proper citations). | 2 | 2 | 3 | 3 | |
| **1.d** | I can provide a concluding statement. | 2 | 2 | 3 | 3 | |
| **Date** | Looking at my data, what's my plan? | | | | | |
| September 26 | I'm still struggling with credible evidence. I'm going to the What I Need (WIN) Time workshop about evidence with Mrs. Perez. | | | | | |

*Source: Adapted from Hansen, 2015a; White Pine Middle School.*

**FIGURE 7.6:** Example of student's progress tracker.

To reap the most benefit from trackers, continually help students self-assess and record their progress. Using trackers consistently is one of the best ways to help students step into their hero role and take ownership of their learning journey. Have them record their progress multiple times—even at the beginning of the unit when they clearly lack proficiency. It's important for learners to see their growth over time so they can tell their story of perseverance. Their tracked progress serves as the evidence for their new story.

> *It's important for learners to see their growth over time so they can tell their story of perseverance. Their tracked progress serves as the evidence for their new story.*

Teachers are often so creative with trackers! I've seen them use race cars and racetracks, sticker charts, simple checkmarks, plus and delta signs, and more. Using a simple numerical representation is often best because it allows students to see their progress over time even more clearly. A simple four-point scale works well to describe where students are on each of the pitfalls (or targets). For example, the score *4* is above proficient (or mastery level), *3* is proficient, *2* is not quite yet proficient, and *1* is far below proficient. What matters much more than which tracking system you use is ensuring learners are actually using the tracker. I do encourage teachers to avoid symbols that represent judgment (like smiley or frowny faces, and especially grades). If a student isn't proficient yet, that's OK. Don't place judgment on students' current position on the journey; instead, provide more opportunities for them to keep trying within their ZPD or prevent pitfalls from tripping up students until they get it. The more learners track their progress, the more they own their progress. Once they do become proficient, say, "You did it! You overcame this hard thing. How'd you do it? What's next?"

> *The more learners track their progress, the more they own their progress.*

## Concluding Thoughts

To help students fully benefit from the Hero-Maker Framework, teachers need some tools. I intentionally kept the directions for building the tools simple. As teachers experience the process and get comfortable thinking differently about their role as leaders of learning and developers of learners, they will take ownership of the process and add complexity and depth to the tools, and more importantly, how they use them.

Still, at first glance, the tools may seem overwhelming among the myriad things on your daily to-do list. So don't try to use these tools for everything you teach. If you do, you may quickly get overwhelmed, frustrated, and quit. But, if you just choose one essential skill to work on at a time in preparation for your next upcoming unit, you can develop what you need in a couple meetings with colleagues or a couple hours on your own.

Some of you will have to let go of your perfectionistic desires to "get it right" on the first iteration. Teachers are on a learning journey too and must give themselves the same level of grace they give students. Besides, if you took a beginner's mindset when you started, you have already accepted that you probably won't get it right the first time anyway. That mindset not only frees you to act quickly but also to make changes and refine your work in your version 2.0, 3.0, and so on. If teachers do the tasks this chapter describes, they will have the basic tools they need to begin helping students take ownership of their learning journey and, ultimately, be the hero in their story.

As helpful as these tools can be, they are only powerful when the person wielding them understands the principles behind the tools. Most importantly, if teachers are going to make these changes of empowerment stick, they must consistently use the tools and apply the Hero-Maker Framework principles. Otherwise, it's too easy to slip back into inherited, traditional roles of teachers being directive and students being compliant. A committed, like-minded team of colleagues working to make these changes together is extremely helpful. Team members can help one another by providing support, accountability, and celebration as they unlearn and relearn how to approach learning and the development of learners.

This chapter is different from the others because it is designed to help with the how-to of the tools. It's necessary because the tools themselves and the process of creating them will help you make some of the shifts in your practice about facilitated feedback, models, rubrics, learning targets, and more. But don't forget, the real aim isn't a few changes in practice and tools or even for the noble purpose of learning more.

Your real aim is to *empower the learners* in your care to trade in their boredom, compliance, or fixed mindsets for ownership, purpose, and self-efficacy. The goal is students' development as powerful individuals. Your purpose is, and always should be, to prepare learners to go out into the world, claim their space, contend, and humbly say (*and mean*):

> I can do hard things. The reason I know I can is because I have done hard things before. It's through my own volition, effort, and perseverance that I have made progress. Even when I get knocked down, I know how to get up and keep trying. I accept responsibility for my trajectory. I am the master of my fate!

This purpose, *the development of your learners*, is your true calling as a teacher and the story you are living.

# EPILOGUE

**W**riting this book has been nothing less than a journey. At times, the challenge of trying to capture my thoughts on the page has felt like wading through deep mud or fighting dragons; it was difficult and truly taxing. It's hard to articulate these concepts on a deep level in a way people will understand and find compelling enough to actually commit to change. But each time I thought one of my dragons had me whooped, I attempted to practice what I preach. I did my best to stand up after getting knocked down in the dirt and continued to fail forward. Sometimes before I could continue, I needed help from a wizard, courage from a loved one, or just a break. I kept trying, failing forward, and doing my best to answer the call I felt to bring the Hero-Maker Framework to the world.

I've done my best to bring these concepts to light in a new way, so people can see and help those students who need it and give them hope for something better. *Hope* is what this book is really all about! It's what so many students and adults need. It's my hope that the Hero-Maker Framework will provide a path for educators to help students each tell a new hope-filled story about themselves, their world (including school), and their place in it.

I also hope the framework helps educators tell a new story about themselves and their role too. I hope it will give educators the collective courage to tell a new story about their fundamental purpose as professionals (that is, moving students away from *learning* content and even specific skills as their most important purpose). Instead, I hope individuals, teams, schools, and even whole systems will have the courage to tell a new story about intentionally empowering learners with the disposition of self-efficacy. It's the disposition of true learners, capable of facing the unknown futures of tomorrow— even the scary, dragon-like challenges guarding the unknown potential buried inside themselves. It's the disposition of a hero. This is your real calling, not just to ensure learning of essential knowledge and skills but also to intentionally *develop the learners themselves*. It's my hope you will boldly declare and live this purpose.

It won't be easy. It starts with letting go of the old stories thrust on educators that hold the teaching profession captive over test scores (along with other archaic metrics for success), which is a fallacy at best and a deception at worst. Scoring 5 percent better on one arbitrary state test designed for the U.S. economy a century ago doesn't make one school better than another today. Educators know this and must not only let go of that story but also no longer allow one single metric to define the story told about educators either, regardless of whether theirs is the "good" school or the "failing" school. No longer can teachers play out the same story with students, forcing compliance with the false reassurance that points, grades, and test scores are the ultimate success and the accumulated currency students need to meet future challenges. Teachers know better! They must rewrite the story for their institution as a system, and their role as teachers. It starts with the kind of stories educators tell themselves.

The stories in this book are more than stories. I tried to tell these stories the way I would if you and I were a couple of friends sharing some food or the warm light of a fire. I used the stories to try to make the practices and principles (which are not really new) come alive in a new way with new depth. But more than teaching practices and principles, stories breathe life into values. Stories give hope. Stories help bridge the gap between the comfort of knowing where you stand and the discomfort of the yet unknown. One reason is because with just a little imagination, stories allow people to step inside and vicariously become part of them. People can and do imagine themselves alongside the characters, acting out the values worth acting out, even if just on a subconscious level. If you try, you can *feel* the experience of what the characters in the stories actually experience. The stories people pay attention to are fundamental to how they shape their perceptions, make sense of the world, and more importantly, how they make sense of themselves in it. Stories shape the journey of people's lives.

And though it seemed as though during this part of my life's journey, I was often battling dragons to write this book, I find myself weirdly not tired, worn out, or needing rest, but instead more resolute, more willing to be vulnerable, more impatient for change, and more affirmed in my declaration that now is the time. It's time to reclaim our profession! It's time for a new story. If we don't change the story about the fundamental purpose of education, who will? Who will fight the growing opinion that attending school for formal education is an obsolete hoop-jumping act of compliance, because anyone can learn anything, anywhere? Educators are the heroes students have been waiting for. Imagine, as part of our new story about the purpose of education, kids will begin telling their own stories about their own development.

Imagine an auditorium filled with family and community members. Learners each tell their story, standing proudly, explaining how their purpose-driven learning led to a new belief in themselves and who they are. They are confident to face challenges (borne out of evidence of experience) and ready to step into the world to own their burden of responsibility. Imagine these learners telling the audience their story, explaining what was hard, where they got knocked down in the dirt, the fearful dragons they had to face, and how they picked themselves up and overcame. They are telling what they learned about themselves as learners and heroes, plus how their transformation applies to their compelling vision for their future. Imagine how touching each of their stories would be. Imagine the tears, cheers, and standing ovations. That's a story worth listening to and a story worth participating in.

The change in students' stories that so many of them need and the fundamental purpose of education start with you as you align and self-actualize your potential and your story. Like a vibrant thread, the transformation weaves in and out of the stories of your learners, holding together a beautiful tapestry that changes the world. Your work intensely matters! If you listen, you will hear the call to become something more—not just a teacher, but a wizard and a hero maker who helps students each assume their rightful role as a learner and a hero. If you listen, you will feel the draw of your potential like a familiar voice (*your future self*) beckoning you to become what you can become. If you listen, face your dragons, and consistently fail forward in your attempts to align with that potential, you will find moments of not only what Maslow (1943) describes as *self-actualization* but also beyond to *self-transcendence*, where your purpose is bigger than you. The framework in this book gives you the tools to begin answering that call.

As I close this journey, I leave you with one last belief I have about stories. To a large degree, adults get to write their own. We don't get to pick the early setting, parts of the plot, or some of the other characters in the story. Sometimes we have no control over the circumstances or events of our lives, but we do get to choose *how we see things*. Adults get to choose whether they align with their potential or not. Some argue that's not true, that circumstances and the constraints we face are bigger than we are and ultimately dictate our choices. Either way, whether adults get to write their story or not, I don't care. I chose to believe they do anyway. I believe adults have choices and those choices individually and collectively write their story.

So, I ask, "What will the rest of your story be? Will you choose to shrink back, let the dragons of fear win, and assume the role of compliant victim, who 'can't,' 'isn't allowed,' or is just 'one cog in the machine?'" Or will you choose to be among the heroes who persevere, consistently pick themselves up out of the dirt to simply try again? Will you constantly realign with who you could be? Will you answer the call to the adventure of your unique potential and assume the weight of responsibility that comes with purpose, just like Zeus burdened the Titan Atlas with the self-transcending weighty purpose of holding the fate of the world on his shoulders? Will you fail forward in the principles of this book, becoming a true and trustworthy wizard for the learners and would-be heroes in your care? Will you tell your story, giving permission for others to do the same, and thus become the catalyst who changes the world? I hope so! I hope this is your hope too. This whole book is about such hopes.

And just like with my last visit with Cody, I want you to know something: I believe in you! And you are more powerful than you think! Good luck as you fail forward in the story of your journey and the story of our shared journey.

# REFERENCES AND RESOURCES

Ainsworth, L. (2003). *"Unwrapping" the standards: A simple process to make standards manageable*. Englewood, CO: Advanced Learning Press.

Ainsworth, L. (2015). *"Unwrapping" the Common Core: A practical process to manage rigorous standards*. West Palm Beach, FL: Learning Sciences International.

Allen, K. A., Gray, D. L., Baumeister, R. F., & Leary, M. R. (2022). The need to belong: A deep dive into the origins, implications, and future of a foundational construct. *Educational Psychology Review, 34*(2), 1133–1156. https://doi.org/10.1007/s10648-021-09633-6

Attia, P. (Host). (2023, April 3). How the brain works, Andrew's fascinating backstory, improving scientific literacy, and more [Audio podcast episode]. In *The Drive*. Accessed at https://peterattiamd.com/andrewhuberman on September 15, 2023.

Bandura, A. (1977). Self-efficacy: Toward a unifying theory of behavioral change. *Psychological Review, 84*(2), 191–215. https://doi.org/10.1037/0033-295X.84.2.191

Bandura, A. (1997). *Self-efficacy: The exercise of control.* New York: Freeman.

Barth, R. S. (2001). *Learning by heart.* San Francisco: Jossey-Bass.

Baumeister, R. F., & Leary, M. R. (1995). The need to belong: Desire for interpersonal attachments as a fundamental human motivation. *Psychological Bulletin, 117*(3), 497–529. https://doi.org/10.1037/0033-2909.117.3.497

BillMoyers.com Staff. (1999, June 18). *The mythology of "Star Wars" with George Lucas.* Accessed at https://billmoyers.com/content/mythology-of-star-wars -george-lucas on October 22, 2023.

Bloom, B. S., Englehart, M. D., Furst, E. J., Hill, W. H., & Krathwohl, D. R. (1956). *Taxonomy of educational objectives: The classification of educational goals (Handbook I: Cognitive domain).* New York: McKay.

Brenneman, R. (2016, March 22). *Gallup student poll finds engagement in school dropping by grade level.* Accessed at https://edweek.org/leadership/gallup -student-poll-finds-engagement-in-school-dropping-by-grade-level/2016/03 on January 30, 2024.

Brooks, C., Carroll, A., Gillies, R. M., & Hattie, J. (2019). A matrix of feedback for learning. *Australian Journal of Teacher Education, 44*(4). https://doi.org /10.14221/ajte.2018v44n4.2

Buffum, A., Mattos, M., & Malone, J. (2018). *Taking action: A handbook for RTI at Work™.* Bloomington, IN: Solution Tree Press.

Campbell, J. (1949). *The hero with a thousand faces.* Princeton, NJ: Princeton University Press.

Cantor, P. (2018). *How does stress affect a child's development and academic potential?* [Video]. YouTube. Accessed at www.youtube.com/watch?v=mWh5jzusVNM on February 1, 2024.

Chappuis, S., Stiggins, R. J., Arter, J., & Chappuis, J. (2004). *Assessment for learning: An action guide for school leaders.* Portland, OR: Assessment Training Institute.

Cherry, K. (2023, December 7). *How to deal with fear of failure?* Accessed at https://verywellmind.com/what-is-the-fear-of-failure-5176202 on January 30, 2024.

Clear, J. (2018). *Atomic habits: An easy & proven way to build good habits & break bad ones*. New York: Avery.

Conley, D. T. (2005). *College knowledge: What it really takes for students to succeed and what we can do to get them ready*. San Francisco: Jossey-Bass.

Conley, D. T. (2010). *College and career ready: Helping all students succeed beyond high school*. San Francisco: Jossey-Bass.

Conversation. (n.d.). In *Merriam Webster's online dictionary*. Accessed at https://merriam-webster.com/dictionary/conversation on March 14, 2023.

Corkindale, G. (2008, May 7). *Overcoming impostor syndrome*. Accessed at https://hbr.org/2008/05/overcoming-imposter-syndrome on September 13, 2023.

Croston, G. (2012, November 29). *The thing we fear more than death: Why predators are responsible for our fear of public speaking* [Blog post]. Accessed at https://psychologytoday.com/us/blog/the-real-story-risk/201211/the-thing-we -fear-more-death on January 30, 2024.

Damon, W. (2008). *The path to purpose: How young people find their calling in life*. New York: Free Press.

Davis, M. (2019, August 9). *Maslow's forgotten pinnacle: Self-transcendence*. Accessed at https://bigthink.com/neuropsych/maslow-self-transcendence on September 13, 2023.

Digital Promise. (2018, August 29). *Research@Work: Supporting students who have experienced trauma* [Video file]. Accessed at https://youtu.be/gNCFWtkDS88 on January 30, 2024.

DuFour, R., DuFour, R., Eaker, R., Many, T. W., & Mattos, M. (2016). *Learning by doing: A handbook for Professional Learning Communities at Work®* (3rd ed.). Bloomington, IN: Solution Tree Press.

DuFour, R., & Marzano, R. J. (2011). *Leaders of learning: How district, school, and classroom leaders improve student achievement*. Bloomington, IN: Solution Tree Press.

Dweck, C. S. (2006). *Mindset: The new psychology of success*. New York: Random House.

Ego. (n.d.) In *Brittanica*. Accessed at www.britannica.com/topic/ego-philosophy-and-psychology on December 29, 2023.

Encourage. (n.d.). In *Online Etymology Dictionary*. Accessed at https://etymonline.com/word/encourage on March 13, 2023.

Flavell, J. H. (1979). Metacognition and cognitive monitoring: A new area of cognitive-developmental inquiry. *American Psychologist, 34*(10), 906–911. https://doi.org/10.1037/0003-066x.34.10.906

Frankl, V. E. (2006). *Man's search for meaning* (H. S. Kushner, I. Lasch, & W. J. Winslade, Trans.). Boston: Beacon Press. (Original work published 1946)

Fullan, M. (2003). *The moral imperative of school leadership*. Thousand Oaks, CA: Corwin.

Geertz, C. (1973). *The interpretation of cultures: Selected essays*. New York: Basic Books.

Gross-Loh, C. (2016, December 16). *How praise became a consolation prize: Helping children confront challenges requires a more nuanced understanding of the "growth mindset."* Accessed at https://theatlantic.com/education/archive/2016/12/how-praise-became-a-consolation-prize/510845 on January 30, 2024.

Guskey, T. R. (2015). *On your mark: Challenging the conventions of grading and reporting*. Bloomington, IN: Solution Tree Press.

Guy-Evans, O. (2023, November 9). *Fight, flight, freeze, or fawn: How we respond to threats*. Simply Psychology. Retrieved from www.simplypsychology.org/fight-flight-freeze-fawn.html

Haines, E. (n.d.). *Dr. Tony Wagner 7 survival skills* [Video file]. YouTube. Accessed at https://youtube.com/watch?v=UXP9UdZ7jsw&t=10s on January 31, 2024.

Hansen, A. (2015a). Co-teaching the RTI and PLC way. In M. Mattos & A. Buffum (Eds.), *It's about time: Planning interventions and extensions in secondary school* (pp. 35–54). Bloomington, IN: Solution Tree Press.

Hansen, A. (2015b). *How to develop PLCs for singletons and small schools*. Bloomington, IN: Solution Tree Press.

Hansen, A. (2017, January 27). *Flexible groups or labeling kids?* [Blog post]. Northeastern Nevada Regional Professional Development Program. Accessed at https://nnrpdp.com/our-blog/flexible-groups-or-labeling-kids on January 30, 2024.

Hansen, A. (2018, August 1). *Owning their learning: Students as partners in next generation rigor* [Conference presentation]. Professional Learning Communities at Work Institute, Lincolnshire, IL.

Hansen, A. (2020, July 1). *In the midst of disruption lies opportunity* [Conference presentation]. Solution Tree Digital Institute (online).

Hattie, J. (2009). *Visible learning: A synthesis of over 800 meta-analyses relating to achievement.* New York: Routledge.

Hattie, J. (2023). *Visible learning: The sequel—A synthesis of over 2,100 meta-analyses relating to achievement.* New York: Routledge.

History.com. (2023). *George Washington Carver.* Accessed at www.history.com /topics/black-history/george-washington-carver on March 29, 2024.

Huberman, A. (2021, September 27). Controlling your dopamine for motivation, focus & satisfaction [Podcast #39]. In *Huberman Lab.* Accessed at www .youtube.com/watch?v=QmOF0crdyRU on January 30, 2024.

Huberman, A. (2022, January 3). The science of making & breaking habits [Podcast #53]. In *Huberman Lab.* Accessed at www.youtube.com/watch?v=Wcs 2PFz5q6g on January 30, 2024.

Jackson, Y. (2011). *The pedagogy of confidence: Inspiring high intellectual performance in urban schools.* New York: Teachers College Press.

Jung, C. G. (1954). *The development of personality* (G. Adler & R. F. C. Hull, Trans.). Princeton, NJ: Princeton University Press.

Jung, C. G. (1980). *The archetypes and the collective unconscious* (2nd ed.). (R. F. C. Hull, Trans.). Princeton, NJ: Princeton University Press. (Original work published 1959)

Katie, B. (2007). *A thousand names for joy: Living in harmony with the way things are.* New York: Harmony Books.

Katie, B., & Mitchell, S. (2008). *Loving what is: How four questions can change your life.* New York: Random House.

Kotler, S. (2014). *The rise of superman: Decoding the science of ultimate human performance.* New York: Houghton Mifflin Harcourt.

Lee, H. (1960). *To kill a mockingbird*. Philadelphia: J. B. Lippincott & Co.

Logan, T. (n.d.). *Why having a vision is the most important aspect of your life.* Accessed at https://consciousmagazine.co/why-having-a-vision-is-the-most-important-aspect-of-your-life/#:~:text=Vision%20gives%20direction%20and%20a,become%20simpler%20and%20more%20meaningful on January 30. 2024.

Marzano, R. J. (2003). *What works in schools: Translating research into action.* Arlington, VA: ASCD.

Marzano, R. J. (2009). *Designing & teaching learning goals & objectives.* Bloomington, IN: Marzano Resources.

Marzano, R. J. (2017) *The new art and science of teaching.* Bloomington, IN: Solution Tree Press.

Maslow, A. H. (1943). A theory of human motivation. *Psychological Review, 50*(4), 370–396.

McKay, C., & Macomber, G. (2023). The importance of relationships in education: Reflections of current educators. *Journal of Education, 203*(4), 751–758. https://doi.org/10.1177/00220574211057044

Mcleod, S. (2023, May 14). *Vygotsky's zone of proximal development and scaffolding.* Accessed at https://simplypsychology.org/zone-of-proximal-development.html on September 15, 2023.

MIT Teaching + Learning Lab. (n.d.). *Help students retain, organize and integrate knowledge.* Accessed at https://tll.mit.edu/teaching-resources/how-to-teach/help-students-retain-organize-and-integrate-knowledge on January 31, 2024.

Muhammad, A. (2015). *Overcoming the achievement gap trap: Liberating mindsets to effect change.* Bloomington, IN: Solution Tree Press.

Over, H. (2016). The origins of belonging: Social motivation in infants and young children. *Philosophical Transactions of the Royal Society B: Biological Sciences, 371*(1686), 20150072. https://doi.org/10.1098/rstb.2015.0072

Piaget, J. (1932). *The moral judgment of the child.* London: Kegan Paul, Trench, Trubner.

Popham, W. J. (2018). *Assessment literacy for educators in a hurry.* Arlington, VA: ASCD.

Psychology Today. (n.d.) *Dopamine.* Accessed at www.psychologytoday.com/us/basics /dopamine#dopamine-and-behavior on January 25, 2024.

Robbins, T. (n.d.). *How can I set compelling goals?* Accessed at https://tonyrobbins .com/ask-tony/can-create-compelling-future on December 21, 2023.

Rogers, C. R. (1951). *Client-centered therapy: Its current practice, implications, and theory.* Boston: Houghton Mifflin.

Rogers, C. R. (1961). *On becoming a person: A therapist's view of psychotherapy.* Boston: Houghton Mifflin.

Schlain, T., & Let It Ripple Studio. (2015, October 8). *The adaptable mind* [Video file]. YouTube. Accessed at https://youtube.com/watch?v=937iCwJd3fI on September 15, 2023.

Schmoker, M. (2011). *Focus: Elevating the essentials to radically improve student learning.* Arlington, VA: ASCD.

Schmoker, M. (2018). *Focus: Elevating the essentials to radically improve student learning* (2nd ed.). Arlington, VA: ASCD.

Scott, S. (2004). *Fierce conversations: Achieving success at work & in life, one conversation at a time.* New York: Berkley Books.

Stiggins, R. J. (2008). *An introduction to student-involved assessment for learning* (5th ed.). Upper Saddle River, NJ: Pearson/Merrill Prentice Hall.

Team Tony. (n.d.). *What's your vision? When you focus on your vision, you're able to accomplish anything.* Accessed at https://tonyrobbins.com/stories/unleash-the -power/focus-on-your-vision/#:~:text=What's%20your%20vision%2C%20 your%20dream,when%20you're%20stressed%20out. on January 31, 2024.

Tolle, E. (2016). *A new earth: Awakening to your life's purpose* (10th anniversary ed.). New York: Penguin.

Vygotsky, L. S. (1986). *Thought and language* (Rev. ed., A. Kozulin, Ed. & Trans.). Cambridge, MA: MIT Press.

Wagner, T., & Dintersmith, T. (2015). *Most likely to succeed: Preparing our students for the innovation era.* New York: Scribner.

Wiggins, G., & McTighe, J. (2005). *Understanding by design* (Expanded 2nd ed.). Arlington, VA: ASCD.

Willcoxon, N., & Marken, S. (2023, June 14). *K–12 schools struggle to prepare, excite Gen Z about learning* [Blog post]. Gallup. Accessed at https://news.gallup.com /opinion/gallup/507053/k12-schools-struggle-prepare-excite-gen-learning.aspx on January 31, 2024.

# INDEX

progress trackers

 doing the work, 77

 examples of a student's progress tracker, 68–69, 118

 examples of a teacher's progress tracker, 67, 116

 facilitated feedback and, 66–69

 Hero-Maker Framework tools and, 106

 for learners, 117–119

 pitfalls on the path to proficiency and, 113–114

 sample kindergarten student progress tracker, 74

 for teachers, 116–117

purpose

 learning goals and, 24

 purpose, meaning, and passion, 52–57

 purpose-driven learning, 57–58

# Q

questions to ask

 helping students create a compelling vision and, 97–99

 questions, tasks, and problems worth talking about, 54–56

# R

recreation and leisure, questions to ask, 98

reflection

 metacognition and, 80, 85

 trusting relationships and, 45–46

visualizing the shift and, 72

rejection, fear of, 38–39

relationships. *See also* leveraging relationships of trust to help students overcome fear

 reflection on, 45–46

 vision and, 97–98

relevance, 8, 51

resistance, 50–51

rigor, 23

Robbins, T., 90

rubrics. *See* descriptions of quality

# S

Scott, S., 48

selecting worthy content to help students develop skills

 about, 47–48

 concluding thoughts, 61

 forced compliance and resistance and, 50–51

 guidelines for selecting, 59

 Hero-Maker Framework and, 15, 47

 purpose, meaning, and passion and, 52–57

 purpose-driven learning and, 57–58

 selecting content for skill development, 58–61

 story about Jentri, 49–50

self-actualization, 57, 123

self-assessment. *See also* facilitating student self-assessment and self-correction

 progress trackers and, 118–119

### How to Develop PLCs for Singletons and Small Schools

*Aaron Hansen*

Ensure singleton teachers feel integrally involved in the PLC process. With this user-friendly guide, you'll discover how small schools, full of singleton teachers who are the only ones in their schools teaching their subject areas, can build successful PLCs.

**BKF676**

### Motivated to Learn

*Staci M. Zolkoski, Calli Lewis Chiu, and Mandy E. Lusk*

In *Motivated to Learn*, you will gain evidence-based approaches for engaging students and equipping them to better focus in the classroom. With this book's straightforward strategies, you can learn to motivate all your students to actively participate in learning.

**BKG037**

### The Independent Learner

*Nina Parrish*

Teach students how to self-regulate with research-affirmed, teacher-tested strategies. This book gives you the tools to support students as they learn how to build intrinsic motivation, emotional literacy, and problem solving—all essential skills for future success.

**BKG017**

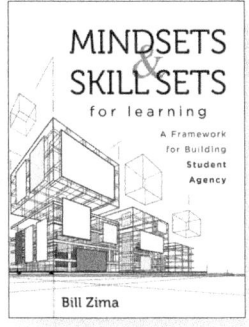

### Mindsets and Skill Sets for Learning

*Bill Zima*

In *Mindsets and Skill Sets for Learning*, author Bill Zima clearly outlines what student agency looks and sounds like in the classroom. Rely on the book's framework to help you create a learner-centered classroom culture and deliberately plan and structure lessons.

**BKL051**

**Solution Tree | Press**

a division of

Solution Tree

Visit SolutionTree.com or call 800.733.6786 to order.